deep
lined
f

REVOLUTION

AS

THEATRE

Robert Brustein

REVOLUTION

AS

THEATRE

notes on the new radical style

LIVERIGHT

NEW YORK

1.987654321

Standard Book Number: 87140–523–3 (cloth)
87140–045–6 (paper)

Library of Congress Catalog Card Number: 70–137867

Designed by Barbara K. Grenquist

Manufactured in the United States of America

For Danny and his future

Contents

Acknowledgments

"Revolution as Theatre" and "The Case for Professionalism" were originally published in the *New Republic* and are reprinted here by permission of the author.

"A Night at the Symposium" is reprinted with permission from the *New York Review of Books.* Copyright © 1969 *The New York Review.*

"When the Panther Came to Yale" and "A Matter of Accountability" were originally published in the *New York Times:* © 1970 by the New York Times Company. Reprinted by permission.

"The Decline of Professionalism" was originally published in *Modern Occasions* and is reprinted by permission of the publisher.

REVOLUTION

AS

THEATRE

1

Introduction

*T*his sampling of essays and articles represents the kind of prose work I have been doing over the past two years. It is not concerned with my customary area of interest, the theatre, except insofar as "theatre" is now a descriptive term for the style of our contemporary culture. I suspect there are those who will advise me to stick to my last, and perhaps they are right. I seem to be growing somewhat polemical in my writing, and the personal note increasingly invades my journalism.

I am no longer simply an observer of theatrical events, but occasionally an unwilling performer as well, and like most actors, I can grow a little too preoccupied with my own role (this explains the material in the appendices). The kind of detachment required for impartial analysis is becoming less and less available in our world — and particularly in the world of the university which has always been its home. If I sound

3

cranky or embattled (as I know I sometimes do), this is because of a growing frustration over many of the things that are happening inside the academy. I am far from alone in this feeling, but it is very rarely expressed openly in the university itself, however often it may be articulated in the world at large. It is a peculiarity of our time that what may be generally accepted among certain segments of society is often an adversary position in the academy, with the result that it becomes more and more difficult for a writer to identify his audience. If I plant myself obstinately into a position already obvious to the reader, this is because I am usually speaking to and about students and faculty — for whom such a position is far from obvious, if it is not considered downright pernicious and antediluvian.

Something is eating me. I have the conviction, and it grows rather than lessens, that we are living in a profoundly decadent society. Worse, I suspect that some of the very things that are taken as symbols of transformation are themselves further signs of decline. Our age is apocalyptic, which means that human or institutional failings of any kind can become the occasion for total refusal, so that whatever is solid and firm in our tradition is abandoned along with whatever is corrupt. A whole century of artists and teachers are being exiled from our memories as if they had never

existed; and in our feverish search for novelty, and our
impatience for change, the trend-setters and fashion-
mongers have usurped the cultural stage. In such a time, our prophets are superseded by trim-
mers, and many are tempted to pander to the hungry
demands of the young. The hard biological truths of
Freud are swallowed up in the squashy social idealism
of the Neo-Freudian revisionists; the dark visions of
D. H. Lawrence are obscured by the writhing motions
of a thousand encounter groups. Newman's idea of
the university as a center for liberal learning is increasingly threatened by demands for "relevance" —
or by a free-floating permissiveness which brings Sum-
merhill to higher education. The heroic individualism
affirmed by Nietzsche and Ibsen is swamped under a
raging new conformity called "community" while the
strong intelligent politics of Marx and Trotsky are
drowned out by the mindless yippie yells of Abbie
Hoffman and Jerry Rubin. We are intimidated by our
avant-garde and deafened by the clamor of indiscriminate protest. We dig vainly for social programs in
romantic revolutionary rhetoric; we scratch for poetry
in the lyrics of folk songs and rock music; and for
philosophy, we turn to those without the patience to
think.

The age is dominated by sentimentality and false
emotionalism; everybody feels compelled suddenly to

demonstrate his good heart. But the humane intelligence is mocked by unconditioned instinct; criticism grows cowardly and patronizing; creative achievement is lost in group demands; and a fickle casualness informs our love. Affluence is employed on behalf of performance, whether by those playing roles of riches or of poverty; and drugs, coercion, and mob action are provided with intellectual justification. Education is used not for the acquisition of knowledge or for the development of the critical temperament, but rather for experiments in life styles, political manipulation, and social engineering, while men of reason founder in a miasma of doubts, uncertainties, and petty surrenders.

Our radicalism, in short, is permeated by many of the failures that characterize our society as a whole. And if I seem to concentrate on the errors of the new radical style, then this is because of a firm conviction that we cannot reverse our present situation until we develop a humane, honest, and intelligible politics. The evils of the present system are certainly obvious enough. The war in Indochina and the inertia of the country in face of serious domestic problems (oppression of the blacks, pollution of the environment, economic deterioration) have weakened our faith in the viability and flexibility of American political institutions. And the Vietnam massacres, the police attacks on the Black Panthers, the gathering threat to rights and liberties, and American support of totalitarian foreign governments have exposed a side of our national character that we used to identify only with fascist regimes. These evils have been sufficiently denounced; in fact, they have been rehearsed so often lately that we are now in danger of producing a melodrama on the stage of American politics where the "Other" — an enemy invariably identified with the "Establishment" — is assumed to be uniquely guilty of cankers that may be ravaging us all.

What is not generally seen or accepted, however, by the radical young and their older supporters is that the "revolutionary" opposition is endowed with a fairly generous share of American brutality, just as the "counter-culture" possesses much of the brainlessness and exploitativeness of the culture as a whole. If we do not continue to preserve high standards for our art (regardless of charges of "elitism"), then we are merely exchanging one form of mediocrity for another; and if we do not try to purify radical politics through frank analysis and honest criticism, then the politics of the country will remain precisely the same, regardless of who takes power. The disease is at the roots. Until we are willing to see how it affects everything and everybody, we are doomed to a repetition of the very errors we are trying to reform.

I submit these notes, then, in the hope that they can make some small contribution to making the radical movement self-conscious. For I share the belief of a number of older men on the Left that a monotonous repetition of self-righteous attacks on the "Other" will result only in a morally repugnant, and politically ineffective, form of false revolutionism (not to mention that sentimental new form of fellow-traveling that Tom Wolfe calls "radical chic"). Events such as Mylai, or the murder of Fred Hampton, or the shooting of Kent State students by the National Guard compel us to go beyond simple expressions of anger and outrage to an examination of how the kinks in the psychological and political machinery of this nation may be short-circuiting us all. Such analyses are important not so we may lose ourselves in banquets of guilt or orgies of masochism, but rather in order to discover the means by which we can transcend our disordered inheritance, and find our way through to workable solutions.

If I am harsh in my critique of the style of young radicals, this is because I feel closer to them than to their antagonists on the Right, and am therefore more despondent when I see them failing their promise. And I am convinced that they are now in deep error, despite their sometimes admirable idealism. For student radicals are now managing, with the aid of certain liberal intellectuals, to institutionalize the innocence that has plagued this country for over a hundred-and-fifty years. When Margaret Mead tells us that the post-war generation has seen the planet in an entirely new way, and is therefore entirely free from taint, what is she doing but creating another myth of the garden, populated by a whole new army of Adams and Eves?

Assigning vices and virtues to whole generations rather than to individuals within those generations helps to keep the American melodrama playing to full houses. So does the willful refusal of past history and knowledge. For the wisdom of the past is important precisely because it helps men overcome their innocence, just as the studies of Freud, Marx, Nietzsche, Lorenz, and countless other original thinkers, are valuable precisely for what they tell us about the darker side of human character. To reject the past wholesale is to doom one-self to be benighted — for until you know yourself in history, you cannot begin to think coherently about the world. The melodrama of the "Other" is a way of perpetuating innocence, just as our glorification of youth is a method of establishing inexperience, anti-intellec-tualism, and the herd instinct as national norms.

The wise men of the Western tribe all have shared a pessimism of the spirit and an optimism of the will.

They have known that the terrible handicaps of human nature could only be overcome through knowledge, discipline, rigor, and hard work. They were willing to accept sacrifice in their development of intelligence, and frustration in their pursuit of truth, because of a shared conviction that only intelligence and truth could set us free, and bring us beyond our natures to the full realization of hopes and ideals.

Of course, I write this out of certain deliberate assumptions, many of which are under severe question at the present time: That human life has value, that the achievement of the artist is one of the highest tokens of existence, that civilization (including Western civilization) is worth preserving, that freedom of thought and opinion is as important to mankind as social and political equality, that wisdom is to be preferred over ignorance. I take it for granted also that the personal, private, and metaphysical side of humanity must be kept free from encroachments by the public and political imperatives of the time, and that the validity of an idea is not necessarily determined by the speed with which it is adopted, or the numbers of those who immediately embrace it. Finally, I believe that courtesy, civility, and decency among human beings are not to be sacrificed even for the highest motives, and that the greatest threat we face today is from totalitarian thinking — both from the right and the left. I have no reason to think that these assumptions are commonly accepted in America today, but I see no hope whatever for any nation that does not make them the basic foundation of its actions and its ideals.

1970

2

Revolution

As

Theatre

The main thing . . . is that the rebellion start off by despising make-believe. . . . If we behave like the other side, then we are on the other side. Instead of changing the world, all we'll achieve is a reflection of the one we want to destroy.

Jean Genet, The Balcony

Amerca seems to be without adequate machinery for the redress of grievances and for social change: It is a measure of this failure that little more is available to those dissatisfied with inequities in the system than ineffective demonstrations against the government, threatening rhetoric, disruptive gestures, and self-conscious life-styles. Partly drained of its resources by an intolerable unending war, partly blocked from progress by an intransigent Administration supported by a selfish white working class, the nation lumbers along in a state of paralysis, unable to move in any direction but the unacceptable one it now pursues. At the same time that grievances accumulate and rage mounts, the government holds absolute power to suppress any insurrection — if not to destroy it from within before it has even begun through an elaborate network of informers.

Partly as a result, meaningful political action is being

15

replaced by radical verbal displays, while revolutionary
agitation has moved from the streetcorners and underground presses to the mass communications media.
What a paradox! America is frequently (and with more
and more cause) charged with being repressive; yet, it
enjoys at present the most extraordinary freedom
of expression in its history, perhaps in the history of
any nation. What is more, this freedom is being used
not just in an infantile way — as in the obscenities of
the confrontationists — or in an experimental way — as
in the current investigations into the boundaries of
pornography — but also in an openly political manner.

Shaw felt compelled to suppress a play as mild as
Heartbreak House until the conclusion of World War I
for fear of arousing the authorities. Today, playwrights
are more likely to shelve their works for fear of dis-
pleasing the revolutionary young. Anti-Vietnam war
plays have become a cliche, and black dramatists indict
white audiences weekly from the stages of Establishment theatres. I can think of no other nation in history,
not even Athens during the time of Aristophanes,
when criticism of a current war and of an established
society has been so open and bitter as at this time,
in this place.

Freedom of this kind ends no wars and fills no
bellies, which is why militant blacks and radical whites
seem so scornful of it. And free speech, even if it lasts,

can hardly be expected to compensate for the economic and political injustices visited upon the poor by the rest of the nation. It is, in fact, of greatest benefit — in our culturally open, politically closed society — to artists and thinkers, a benefit that may show some returns when they once again begin to create and think. Still, militants and radicals have been quick to take advantage of these extended verbal freedoms, despite their expressed contempt for them — largely as a result of the new hospitality being offered to radical expression by newspapers, magazines, television, radio, and publishing houses. Given their past record of conformist thought and engineered consent (a record I observed without much hope in 1961 in "The Madison Avenue Villain"*), the media have been astonishing in their new openness to a wide spectrum of political opinion. Indeed, this may be the real reason why they have been subjected to such abuse recently by the Yahoos of the Administration.

The Administration, however, need not worry, for little has come out of these appearances except entertainment. Instead of using their opportunities for the formulation of radical ideas and innovative programs,

---

* "The Madison Avenue Villain" was first published in the *Partisan Review* in 1961 and later republished in a collection of my essays entitled *The Third Theatre*.

the media revolutionaries have instead been indulging in muscle-flexing and tub-thumping, proclaiming their violent plans on all the major talk shows, between the commercials and before and after the Late Show. It is odd, to say the least, to find revolutionaries broadcasting their intentions, including their intention to overthrow the system, to such a wide audience. In the past, revolutionaries have been rather less publicity-minded, choosing to remain anonymous except when they wished to win over more followers to an ideology or program. What this violent talk signifies is that American revolutionaries are impotent to act, and that they lack an ideology entirely, though they are hardly lacking in passions — thus, the weakness for rhetoric and gestures, rather than programs and organization.

The result is not revolution but rather theatre — a product of histrionic personalities and staged events — which may explain why a drama critic has the temerity to scrutinize it. When James Forman disrupts a church service to demand reparations from Episcopalians or when Sonny Carson and his followers, Mace in hand, grab the microphones at a Regional Plan Association meeting discussing New York's master plan, then we know that the incidents have been staged for the newspaper reporters and television cameras and should, therefore, be more properly evaluated by aesthetic than by political criteria, according to the quality of the dialogue, costumes, acting, and direction. Although it may be argued that such incidents are dress rehearsals rather than actual performances (and therefore should not be prematurely judged) the truth is that many of these performances will never take place — only endless previews before a safe audience that can be counted upon to tolerate the charade, if not actually to applaud it.

I do not mean to deny that some of these performers may eventually expose themselves to danger — that they may, in Genet's words, "be so carried away by their passions that they no longer recognize anything, and leap, without realizing it, into . . . reality." The Weathermen, the Young Lords, and the Black Panthers certainly have the capability to transform their rhetoric into violent action, and are now suffering the consequences in even more violent official retaliation (in the Chicago trial, the rhetoric alone resulted in terrible judicial overkill). Still, both actions and rhetoric are an extension of theatricality, and proceed through the impulse to impersonate. When the Weathermen lock arms down a Chicago street, chanting "We love our uncle, Ho Chi Minh," or when the Young Lords play at being Che Guevara and Castro, or when the Panthers, in paramilitary costumes, have their pictures taken giving breakfast to ghetto children, then the link with public relations and playacting becomes obvious. In-

deed, the alleged murder of an alleged Panther informer
in New Haven bore sufficient similarities to the plot
of a recent movie (Jules Dassin's *Uptight*, a remake
of *The Informer*, revolving around black revolutionaries) to make one suspect that life was imitating art.

Some newspapers concede the theatrical aspect of
the revolution by publishing articles by its more cele-
brated figures in the amusement pages (it is note-
worthy that these figures are often theatre celebrities).
The *New York Times*, for example, can usually be
expected to invite LeRoi Jones or Ed Bullins, or one
of their followers, to do a black avenger routine every
other Sunday in its drama pages — where they will
dutifully froth away at the "white beasts" and declare
their intention to murder and enslave them. The occasion for these fulminations is customarily the opening
of a new play in some blazing revolutionary haunt like
the Brooklyn Academy of Music where the playwright's work will be mechanically praised, regardless
of its merit, first by a white reviewer (or by a black
one, if the other offers the slightest reservation), and
then by an audience composed largely of guilty white
liberals — thus providing the playwright with royalties,
ostensibly to purchase arms for the extermination of
the society that is applauding his work.

This bewildering habit of claiming social rewards for
revolutionary activity can be observed more closely in

the progress of a career like James Kunen's. After participating in the occupations at Columbia in 1967 and in the bust that followed, Kunen recorded his experiences in a slim volume called *The Strawberry Statement*. There he was able to testify to his deep and abiding alienation from American life. American life responded by offering him wide praise and considerable fame, not to mention the inevitable invitations from mass magazines and TV talk shows, where he used the opportunity to bristle even more fiercely over the corruptions of the capitalistic ethic. It didn't take long before Hollywood had bought his book for an undisclosed sum, and MGM began to make a movie of it — with James Kunen playing one of the roles! Recently, Kunen pondered, in another glossy magazine, about the morality of his involvement with the film, as well as on "the irony of 1.9 million dollars being spent to make a movie about a protest against the works of capitalism." His conclusion: that making Hollywood movies about revolution is really the same as making revolution.

Developments of this kind are inevitable in a culture where fame is replacing money as the animating drive of ambitious men and the cardinal sign of achievement. ("In five years," as Andy Warhol has cogently observed, "everybody in the world will be famous for fifteen minutes.") And one of the current formulas for finding fame is theatricalized revolution — revolution for the hell of it — designed to capture attention for an individual through some extraordinary antic. This impulse may help account for the mindlessness of the movement, and may explain why radical thinkers like Christopher Lasch, Paul Goodman, Eugene Genovese, Bayard Rustin, and Irving Howe are such isolated figures these days, and so unpopular with the revolutionary young. When performance is considered more important than the script, hard economic solutions and practical programs are abandoned for mass media confrontations which lead nowhere except to further publicity. In place of thought, we are given expletives and imprecations, used so indiscriminately that they have lost their meaning even for those who employ them. And what may have been originally stimulated by a desire to dramatize a cause for the sake of curing an injustice now often seems like theatre for its own sake, destructive in its aim, negative in its effect, performed with no particular end in mind.

The compulsion to act out revolutionary moral concerns is hardly confined these days to militants and radicals: It is shared by successful, wealthy liberals as well. The age has spawned a new hybrid: the cocktail party revolutionary. Trailing excitement through the corridors of universities, museums, courtrooms, and publishing houses, always certain (in Saul Bellow's words) to enact his "revolutionary passions against a background of institutional safety," he dreams fantasies of violence within a context of hedonism, usually stopping short of physical danger or property loss. In Pancho Villa moustaches and granny glasses, long hair flowing over his maxicoat, the cocktail party revolutionary works feverishly to establish his alliance, through speech, clothes, and style, with the radical theatrics of the day. Nothing testifies more to the fashionableness of the movement than his involvement with it, for he is the style-spotter and trend-setter of the time.

Thus, we find New York hostesses transferring their charitable impulses from the Junior League and the hospital fund to the Black Panthers and other radical groups — raising money, over cocktails and canapes, to help such movements achieve their objectives. (Obviously, I am not criticizing the sincere efforts of serious civil liberties groups to protect the physical safety and civil rights of radicals threatened with police violence and legal harassment.) There is something profoundly disturbing about the moral spectacle of these affairs, when guests file past private guards or through these intricate safety systems that have become so common in Manhattan today to be exhorted by those whose announced aims include the abolition of private property and the extermination of the "pigs."

It would be interesting to know how quickly the police would be called were one of these Panthers to enter a townhouse without an invitation to address the assembled guests.

Thus, we find the sons and daughters of the wealthy contributing portions of their inherited patrimony — not to aid the poor and oppressed, but to underwrite the bail of men and women accused of bombing government buildings. (One wonders if this generosity was inspired by a presumption of innocence — or of guilt.) Thus, we are treated to a television special starring Simon and Garfunkel, organized less around their music than around their feelings about the state of society — describing their alienation to hordes of swooning admirers, and singing their urban folk songs to the accompaniment of film clips showing war, poverty, and protest marches. What portion of their royalties, one wonders, has gone to Resist and the Urban Coalition? Thus, we come upon a Broadway production of *Indians* which invites the audience, at ten dollars a throw, to feel indignation over the exploitation of the American redman, while exploiting the Indian almost as ruthlessly for the sake of the theatrical spectacle. What percentage of the gross was intended for the Sioux?

Moral posturing of this kind, unaccompanied as it is by risk or difficulty, is a sure sign of sentimentality

— and nowhere is the sentimentalist more conspicuous these days than in the university. There students protest bourgeois materialism by consciously adopting the life-styles of the under classes, while at the same time expending enormous sums on electronic equipment, records, rock concerts, costumes, and drugs. The more radical students identify themselves with dining hall workers, protesting their long hours and low pay, while continuing to eat and live in college comfort without lifting a finger to help them with the trays. Others express their fury over the brutalities of the ROTC program by swarming over university buildings and holding officials prisoner, if not by throwing firebombs through the windows of ROTC offices — in the early hours, to be sure, when nobody but the night watchman is liable to be killed. Still others communicate their sense of bondage through countless "liberation fronts," representing such oppressed groups as undergraduates, postgraduates, women, and dormitory residents. (How hard it is for the young to express themselves without forming into movements or groups). It is the age of the seething grievance, when everyone is joining an undifferentiated chorus of complaint on so many subjects that one is hard put to separate out the real from the phony issues.

And then there is rock music — the perfect emblem of revolutionary theatre: turbulent, deafening, convulsive, stoned, communal, both popular and special, at the same time electronic and anti-technological, endlessly affluent and endlessly alienated. From the photos of the innumerable groups that glower hairily from record covers, you would never guess how fabulously profitable the rock business has become or how vast is its potential for exploiting simulated poverty and rural affectation. Rightly praised at first for its accomplishments as a strong popular expression, and then elevated (with the help of intellectual critics) into the ranks of an "artform," if not a form of religious salvation, rock music has been suffering from self-importance ever since. Lately, it also has been suffering from an increasing brutalization. One thinks of the Rolling Stones being protected from overzealous admirers by a bodyguard of knife-wielding Hell's Angels; or of Jimi Hendrix, pulverizing his guitar in a frenzy of musical emotion (an endless supply of instruments, naturally, awaits him in the wings)*; or of a Michigan group called the Up whose members carry rifles and place bayonets on their guitars. Much of rock music, in short, is carried along on waves of violence, and it inspires violent dreams in its listeners. As one rock critic recently phrased it, after suggest-

---

* Since this was written, Jimi Hendrix died as a result of suffocation brought on by vomiting, presumably from an overdose.

ing that a rock opera called *Tommy* should be performed at the Metropolitan Opera House: "The evening's proceeds would be donated to purchase bombs for needy high school students. After all, Verdi's *Ernani* sparked a revolution in Italy — why shouldn't *Tommy* trigger the first gun of the American revolution from that citadel of uptightness, the Met?"

Clearly, we are suffering from a serious dissociation between our language and its implications: It is as if nobody hears what he is saying any more. One's impulse is to dissolve in pure disgust, but Timon's way leads nowhere either. What to do? Stranded between two ignorant armies, each dedicated to obliterating the other, each identifying everyone else as the enemy, how does one defend the integrity of the truth and the foundation of humane values? We can make a small beginning, I think, by conceding that *revolution* in America is a stage idea, and turning away from these playactors of the ideal. This means writing off the radical extremes of the current younger generation and trying to cultivate the genuine warmth and decency that this generation still retains. For the extremists have failed us badly. We had looked for intelligence as well as passion, programs as well as postures, kindness as well as zeal, and what we got was make-believe, ambition, fashion, self-indulgence, and incredible self-righteousness. We discovered that idealistic Americans

were also violent Americans, and that for all the moral
superiority of the revolutionaries to the Establishment,
they were creating a mirror image of the society they
wished to overthrow. The only revolution barely possible under present circumstances is a revolution of
character, and this can be initiated only through an
act of moral transcendence, humane intelligence, and
deliberate will. It is a small enough hope, but without it, I am afraid, we will remain lost in the mirror,
frozen on the stage, forever blocked off from the reality
of meaningful change.

1970

3

A Night

at the

Symposium

As a benefit for
itself, the Theatre for Ideas had organized a symposium
on the subject *Theatre or Therapy*. In the expecta-
tion of a large turnout, a capacious hall had been hired
near Gramercy Square called The Meeting House. It
was a handsome room with a three-sided balcony and
a platform consisting, like the auditorium, of pews —
a good atmosphere for rational discussion. Shirley
Broughton, director of the Theatre for Ideas, had invited me to participate in the symposium, and I had
accepted, in spite of a hectic schedule, an instinctual
distaste for such affairs, and an ominous sense of fore-
boding.

I had recently published an article on the Living
Theatre in the *New York Review* in which I criticized
the company, along with some elements of the radical
young, for mindlessness, humorlessness, and romantic
revolutionary rhetoric. Since the directors of the Liv-

ing Theatre, Judith Malina and Julian Beck, were also
invited to the symposium, along with Paul Goodman
and Nat Hentoff (who was to serve as moderator), the
meeting looked to me like a good opportunity for more
extended debate on these questions, as well as for ex-
ploring the differences between those who practiced
the "new theatre" and those more skeptical about its
aims and aspirations. On the other hand, I had been
hearing rumors that attempts would be made to dis-
rupt this symposium. Since I don't function too well
under disruptive conditions, I thought it wise to make
some notes, rather than run the risk of trying to ex-
temporize during a heckling session.

Because of difficulty with the sound system — a
difficulty never adequately repaired — the symposium
began a half hour late. I took the opportunity to re-
new my acquaintance with Hentoff and Goodman,
and with the Becks whom I had not seen since their
visit to Yale last fall. The Becks seemed amiable,
though a little breathless, and talked about their
American tour, then in its final week. Non-violence
was in trouble, they said. The "revolution" was going
beyond pacifism on the assumption that only violent
overthrow of the Establishment could cure its in-
eradicable insanity and corruption. I wondered if the
Becks, too, had rejected the non-violence which they

always declared to be the basis for their anarchistic program.

Hentoff worried about the proper order of the speaking, Goodman about the meaning of the topic. We decided to limit our statements to ten minutes each, then to debate each other, and then to throw the debate open to the audience. We were also cautioned — with myself speaking first, Goodman second, and the Becks last — to make some effort to interpret the vague topic title in the course of our statements.

We entered the hall past an audience that was growing restive. I caught sight of a number of friends in the house, also a number of *Le Living* stationed in the balcony and the orchestra. Hentoff started to introduce the discussion — into a dead mike. We whistled and spoke numbers into our equipment, and when it finally seemed in comparatively good working order, we were able to begin.

Hentoff reflected on the confusing nature of the subject we were discussing, and asked me to attempt a definition. I did so, speaking from my notes, after mumbling some apology for the insecurity that had prompted them:

"*Theatre or Therapy* is a rather loaded topic title," I said, "but it does begin to indicate the kind of controversy that is occupying the theatre today where the central question seems to be: To what extent should a production be oriented toward the audience, to what extent toward the actors, and to what extent toward the playwright? One's answer to this is affected by one's attitude toward some important issues of our time: Freedom versus responsibility, activist theatre versus non-activist theatre, free improvisation versus disciplined skill, process versus presentation, and so forth."

A voice from the balcony: "What the hell is disciplined skill?"

A voice from the orchestra: "Shut up, you twerp."

From the balcony: "Fuck you, I'm asking him a question."

From the orchestra: "We'll listen to you later. He's doing the talking now."

"My own position quite simply stated is this," I continued. "I believe the theatre to be served best when it is served by supremely gifted individuals possessed of superior vision and the capacity to express this in enduring form. In short, I believe in the theatre as a place for high art."

The heckler: "We're all supremely gifted individuals."

Brustein: "I doubt that very much."

The heckler: "Up against the wall."

I decided to skip the repartee and get through the

statement. "I do not believe the theatre changes anybody, politically or psychologically, and I don't believe
it should try to change anybody. While necessarily
concerned with social-political as well as psychological-
metaphysical issues, the theatre cannot be expected to
resolve these issues. . . . Chekhov, one of those supremely gifted individuals I spoke of, has said. . ."

"Fuck Chekhov!"

". . . that the correct presentation of problems, and
not the solution of problems, is what is obligatory for
the artist." I elaborated on this notion, describing how
democratic America — and now "revolutionary" America — had always been uncomfortable with the concept
of high art because of its elitist and aristocratic implications. Now the practitioners of the "new theatre"
have joined the old Philistines in the scandalous
American contempt for art.

I concluded: "We are at the tail end of Roman-
ticism when the spectators are on the stage, and actors
are refusing to play roles that are not sufficiently close
to their own personalities. The rationale behind this
reluctance is a refusal of external limitations — limitations which are now called 'authoritarian.' This direction was already anticipated in the work of the Actors
Studio whose members were encouraged to examine
not the lives of the characters they played but rather
their own psychic eccentricities with the result that

the actors invariably played themselves rather than
their roles. Under such conditions, why use actors at
all? This is an extension of America's love of amateurism, and looks forward to a time when there will be
no more spectators, only performers — *arrogant, liberated amateurs, each tied up in his own tight bag.*"

I aimed these last phrases at the heckler in the balcony, though he had been relatively silent during the
last part of my statement.

Paul Goodman spoke next — without notes. He rem-
inisced affectionately about the past work of the
Living Theatre company, particularly its productions
of *The Connection*, of Brecht, and of his own plays.
He had enjoyed my *New York Review* article, he
said, but he couldn't understand what I was so "hot
and bothered" about — he confessed that he had seen
none of the work of the Living Theatre on its recent
tour. Goodman then proceeded to draw an analogy
between contemporary unrest and the Protestant
Reformation.

"Don't think you're like the Christians in the cata-
combs," he said. "You're not going to destroy the
institutions, you're going to reform them. You talk
like there's a cataclysm coming, but there isn't. . . .
The institutions will survive. . . ."

"No, they won't," shouted Rufus Collins, a black
member of the company who had suddenly mate-

rialized on the floor of the hall. "Because we're going to destroy them."

"You're not going to destroy them," replied Goodman, goodhumoredly. "You can't destroy them. And you won't even reform them unless you can think up some ideas. I've lived through movements like this before, and I'm always struck by the poverty of ideas. In two thousand years, there hasn't been a single new revolutionary idea."

"We'll destroy them," screamed Collins, hysterically. "We'll create a cataclysm."

"You're not powerful enough. You're just an idiosyncratic fringe group like the Anabaptists. You don't have the capacity even to close down the universities."

"Close them down, close them down," shrilled Collins. "Fuck the universities!"

"If you start to do that," affirmed Goodman, still maintaining his sweet reasonableness, "they'll just put you on a reservation somewhere and keep you quiet."

"They're going to put us on reservations and kill us," raged Collins, his voice now cracking with fury. "They're going to exterminate us, just like the Indians — the racists, the genocides. They're going to kill all of us."

"No, they won't," answered Goodman. "They'll just feed you some LSD and keep you pacified."

Norman Mailer chose to make his entrance at this point, lumbering down the aisle to his seat just as Goodman was replying to one of Rufus Collins' assaults on America's machine culture.

"Don't blame everything on technology," Goodman said. "It's too easy. Just the other day, I listened to a young fellow sing a very passionate song about how technology is killing us and all that. . . . But before he started, he bent down and plugged his electric guitar into the infrastructure."

Collins was livid, and began jumping up and down in a tantrum. "That boy has thrown away his guitar. He's taken off his clothes. He's going up to the mountains where he's using only his voice and his feet. Fuck technology!"

"Why are you wearing glasses, then?" asked a man near him.

"BECAUSE I CAN'T SEE," screamed Collins. "FUCK TECHNOLOGY! FUCK TECHNOLOGY!"

Mailer applauded loudly and conspicuously. Goodman shrugged and sat down on the floor in front of his seat with his back to the audience. He lit up his pipe, and listened attentively to Judith Malina who spoke next.

But the mike was dead again. "Turn her microphone on," urged Hentoff to the sound man. "Yes," said Miss Malina, "turn me on." Pleased with her witticism, she repeated it a few times. "Am I turned on? Okay. . ."

"Bob Brustein said something about freedom and responsibility, like they were different things. This is all tied up with questions I don't want to get into tonight, like are we good or bad at heart. I do want to say that when people act freely, with complete freedom, they act creatively, beautifully. Everybody has it in him to be an artist — there's no such thing as special individuals who are supremely gifted. When the audience does its thing in *Paradise Now*, it does some wild, beautiful, creative scenes. Not always, of course, but I've seen people do things as beautiful as I've ever seen in the theatre. Better than us . . . better than Shakespeare or Euripides. . . ."

"Fuck Shakespeare. Fuck Euripides," yelled the balcony voice.

"I dig Shakespeare sometimes," Miss Malina replied. "But I also want to speak in my own voice, in my own person. I mean there's Hedda Gabler and there's Judith Malina, and I want to be Judith Malina."

"Let's have five minutes of Hedda Gabler," shouted one of the spectators in the orchestra pews. "We've already had five minutes of Judith Malina."

"I'll give you Hedda Gabler," yelled the heckler in the balcony, adding in a mincing voice, " 'The candle is on the table.' That's Hedda Gabler. Now I'll give you me: Fuck Ibsen. Fuck all liberal intellectuals and their fucking discussions. . . ."

"Another thing," Judith Malina said. "The first night we did *Paradise Now* at Yale — the night we got busted — we all came out of the theatre on each other's shoulders and into the streets. It was a very beautiful and joyous moment, everybody was feeling like something beautiful was happening. And Bob Brustein came up to me and said: 'Judith, I hate this play. All this freedom, it could lead to fascism.' But I said, freedom is beautiful. It can never lead to fascism, it can only lead to more freedom."

This remark was the cue for pandemonium; the entire Living Theatre company proceeded to take over the Meeting House. A flamboyant actor named Olé, dressed in yards and yards of brightly colored silk, snaked onto the platform where he began doing fashion model poses while sucking on a long thin cigar. Rufus Collins on the floor of the auditorium was joined by Stephen Ben Israel (the heckler from the balcony) where both started shouting obscenities at the audience. Jenny Hecht almost broke her neck climbing down from the balcony, her electrified hair shooting wildly in every direction. Other actors from *Le Living* began pounding on the railings and screaming at the top of their lungs. And now the audience began to scream back.

Shirley Broughton came running down the aisle, toying with strategies, wondering whether or not to return everybody's money. Hentoff conferred with her about the possibilities of moderating the tumult, decided against it, and leaned back to watch the spectacle. Goodman attempted for a while to discuss issues with the actors, the audience, and the Becks. Shouted down, he walked calmly off the platform and out of the hall, puffing on his pipe.

Rufus Collins was screaming: "You people all came here to have one of your discussions. Ten dollars you paid to get in here. We'll give you ten dollars worth."

"How did you get in? What about your ten dollars?"

"I got in for nothing. I don't pay for shit like this. Your money came out of my black skin and the skin of my black brothers. My own mother couldn't come here tonight. She called up and was told she couldn't attend your fucking meeting. That's when I decided to come. . . ."

Stephen Ben Israel was holding a purse high over his head. "That lady over there hit me with her pocketbook — so I took it away from her. And this is what I am going to do with that pocketbook." He opened the purse, held it upside down high over his head, and emptied its contents on the floor.

A voice from the back, calm, sweet, and patient: "I

just embraced eight members of the Living Theatre.
I embraced them with love. And one of them took my
wallet. You can keep the money, but would you kindly
return the cards?"

"*Credit* cards? To buy things in this fucking money
culture? Tear up the cards! Tear up the cards! Burn
the money!"

Julian Beck, above the din: "Coming attractions.
This is happening all over America, in every meeting
house in America. Coming attractions. This is what is
going to happen from now on."

Ben Israel was now on the platform, chanting
verses from R.D. Laing: "If I could turn you on, if I
could drive you out of your wretched mind. . . ."

Collins was yelling into the microphone: "Do the
Africans have theatre? When they beat their drums
and do their dances? Do the Latin Americans have
theatre? Do the Cubans have theatre? Do the Viet-
namese have theatre? I want Brustein to answer yes
or no."

"Yes," I shouted. By this time, I was off the platform and sitting with friends.

A woman in a fur stole pushed her way to the platform toward Rufus Collins, shouting: "You're rude,
you're stupid, and you're vulgar. People paid money
to come here and listen to a discussion and you. . . ."
A young man came up behind her and started pin-

ning an obscene message on the back of her stole. A
spectator came up and pulled the message off. She
continued her conversation with Julian Beck who
asked her: "Why are you wearing that loathsome
fur?"

"To keep me warm."

"You musn't wear the skins of animals," answered
Beck. "It's disgusting," and he tore the stole off her
shoulders.

"Tell your followers not to wear sheepskins then,"
the woman said, picking her fur off the floor.

"I tell them all the time," replied Beck, ripping
her hat off her head and sending it to the floor.
"What are you doing about Vietnam? What are you
doing for the black people?"

"Today I marched in Newark," the woman said,
getting very angry. "I am a poet, and I am as out-
raged as you over the treatment of the blacks in this
country."

"It's not enough, it's enough," said Beck. He was
shouting in her ear and spraying her with his anger.

"I feel hate," said the woman in a low voice. "Today I feel more hate than I have ever felt in my life.
I'm going home now. I'm going to write a poem
about the hate I feel for you."

Now Richard Schechner was on the platform,
fondling one of the mikes. He sat crosslegged, smiling.

With his moustache, long hair, and striped tee shirt, he looked like an Apache dancer. "You've all got to try to understand this," he said to the angry audience. "You've got to learn to groove with it. Let's all have five minutes of meditation to think about the beautiful thing that's happening here."

I shouted, "Tell it like it is, Dick." I was beginning to enjoy myself.

The din in the Meeting House was bouncing off the walls, like a bad mix in a recording studio. Everyone was wandering around the hall, shouting at each other. Two private cops, both of them black, came into the room, trying to look friendly and relaxed. They were mostly concerned with preventing any smoking in the hall.

Suddenly, the wave of bodies in the aisle parted. Norman Mailer had risen, and was strutting towards the platform, pitching and rolling like a loaded freighter in a heavy sea. He was wearing a well-tailored blue suit with a vest, and his face was flushed. He grabbed one of the mikes.

"I was one of those that applauded when Mr. Black over there said 'Fuck Technology' — so I'm not going to use this thing." He laid the mike on the pew beside him. "I'm forty-six years old. I've got a strong voice, but I don't want to waste it. So I want

you all to listen, and listen hard." Some of the tumult
subsided.

"This is a tough town," Mailer continued in his
stacatto manner, "the toughest town in the world.
Because if you think you're tough, there's always
somebody who's tougher. Remember that!" The
tumult was beginning again. "Now I've got a message
for Mr. Black over there. You've got no surprises, and
you haven't had any since the French Revolution.
I've seen all this *jacquerie* before, many times before.
Get it? J-a-c-q-u-e-r-i-e. It's a pun in case you don't
know it." The pun was lost on most of the audience
that was listening, including me.

Ben Israel grabbed a mike and began topping Mailer:
"You should have sent your suit up there Mailer, and
stayed home yourself." Collins started screaming.
Mailer remained on the platform for a short while, a
faint hard smile on his face, trying to stare down his
noisy antagonists. Then he said, "I guess I lost Round
One," and left the platform.

About a third of the spectators had drifted out by
this time. Some wandered into the back room where
drinks and sandwiches were being served. Paul Goodman had returned to the hall and was arguing with
Rufus Collins who told him: "I don't take drugs to
escape from reality. I take drugs to reach reality."

Hentoff remained on the platform, a weary witness. Saul Gottlieb, producer of the Living Theatre's American tour, was talking gently into a microphone.

"I want Bob Brustein to say why he thinks the Living Theatre is fascist."

Saul is a portly, stooped man with a fuzzy beard, a veteran of many ideological wars. I went up to the platform and gave him a kiss.

Judith Malina now had a mike and was walking back and forth in front of her husband like a jaguar.

"I think what happened here tonight was beautiful and good," she said. "You've had an experience — like you've never had before. This is what we should all be discussing now, how beautiful this evening was. How many people here think it was beautiful?"

"Sit down, sit down," came a voice from the hall. "You may think it's beautiful, but it's not what we came for. The subject was Theatre or Therapy, and all we got tonight was therapy — Living Theatre therapy. When do we get to listen to some discussion about theatre?"

"This is better than discussion, better than theatre," replied Miss Malina. "It's spontaneous, it's authentic, it's beautiful, it's real. There seem to be two groups here," she continued, "those who think this is beautiful and those who think it's ugly. Let's find out how many of each."

Stanley Kauffmann was on his feet, and it was the only time in our friendship I had ever seen him angry. "There's a third group," he shouted, "those who think it was planned, rehearsed, and *phony, phony, phony.*"

"No, no," cried Judith Malina. "We allow our people to do just what they want to do. Everybody should be allowed to do what he wants. That's what's so beautiful about freedom."

"You talk about *freedom!*" somebody else shouted over the din. "What about *our* freedom? We weren't allowed to have what we paid for. Your freedom is our repression!"

Julian Beck, who had been sitting all this time like a guru, silent and withdrawn, suddenly stood up. "Coming attractions," he said. "It's happening all over the country. And it will happen again and again whenever you try to hold a meeting. Coming attractions."

*   *   *

In one of the Marx Brothers movies, there is a scene in which Harpo picks up a book, looks it over very carefully, and then goes into a blind fury, tearing

the book to bits and jumping up and down on the
pages and the binding.

Groucho: "What's the matter with him?"

Chico: "He gets angry because he can't read."

1969

4

When the Panther

Came

to Yale

I

When all the tumult began at Yale over the New Haven trial of the Black Panthers, I was deep into rehearsals for a production of *Don Juan* at the Yale Repertory Theatre. The conjunction of events seemed to me significant at the time, and nothing that followed was to alter my sense of tortured symbolic contrasts. Social and political issues were helping to mobilize the campus toward a commitment that declared all other activity "irrelevant," and here we were proceeding with the provocative business of trying to formulate works of theatrical art — from another century and civilization, no less.

This uneasy confrontation of culture by politics — of free expression by social action — was occurring in the classroom as well. On the morning that a minority of radical students had decreed a three-day moratorium on academic activity so that the university might dis-

51

cuss the fate of the Panthers, I was holding a seminar with thirteen Doctor of Fine Arts students from the School of Drama on John Webster's Jacobean tragedy, *The White Devil.* A student report was in progress when through the open window climbed an undergraduate from the Branford Liberation Front (a radical cadre of students from the residential college in whose oak-paneled Fellows Room our seminar was being held).

"What can we do for you?" I asked.

"You shouldn't be holding classes today," the student replied. "You should be talking and thinking about the Panthers and how to free Bobby Seale."

"Should?" I said.

"There's a reality happening out there," the student replied. "And you should be dealing with it."

"There's a reality in here too," I answered. "There are twenty-four hours in each day — our seminar meets two hours a week — so there's plenty of time left for political activity without interrupting us."

One of my students asked the young man to sit down and join the class. He listened to the report for about ten minutes, possibly under the illusion that a "white devil" had something to do with racism, and then left by the door. We spent the rest of the period anxiously wondering whether we might soon be entertaining a larger, more coercive group of visitors.

A few days later, the pressures on everyone increased. On April 21st, the Moratorium Committee called a mass meeting in Ingall's Rink for the purpose of shutting down the entire university in sympathy with the Panthers who were on trial. All presumption of guilt or innocence in the alleged murder of Alex Rackley, whose tortured and mutilated body had been discovered in Middlefield swamp in the spring of last year, was now being swallowed up in the general indignation caused by the legal harassment and police suppression of Panthers throughout the nation, the extradition of Bobby Seale from Chicago to stand trial on a murder charge in New Haven, and, most recently, the six-month contempt-of-court sentences handed out by the presiding judge to David Hilliard and Emory Douglass, two Panther officials, for minor infractions of courtroom rules (both sentences were suspended when the men apologized to the court). The May 1st weekend was approaching, with its ominous promise of violent action from both radical left and rabid right, and students were obviously anxious to express their sympathy with the New Haven Nine. They were also anxious to prevent Yale from becoming a primary target of a growing rage. Just a week before, some Panther speakers had urged Yale students to demonstrate their revolutionary commitment by getting guns and occupying

Beinecke Library, where the university stored its rare
books.

The turnout at Ingall's was huge — the estimate was
4500 — with every bleacher in the hockey rink and
most of the playing space crammed with excited students and faculty, as well as wandering reporters carry-
ing movie cameras and tape recorders. On the visitor's
side of the rink a platform had been placed, fifteen
feet long and four feet wide, facing most of the spectators, while directly behind the platform, in a reserved section of the bleachers, sat the black faculty
and students in a group. Unlike a similar meeting last
spring, when university members met to consider the
question of ROTC on campus, this meeting was not
open to discussion or to votes. It was organized rather
as a series of exhortations delivered by Panther officials, black faculty, black students, black community
representatives, and representatives of other groups,
designed to support a culminating call for a university-
wide strike.

The nominal chairman of the meeting was a black
graduate student in philosophy, Gilbert Rochon, but
its animating force was Kenneth Mills, a young Assist-
ant Professor of Philosophy. Trinidad-born, Oxford-
educated, Mills is an inordinately tall man with a
burst of hair that stands upright on his head, giving
him an immense, imposing presence. An extremely

skilled debater and Marxist theoretician with a langorous, mellifluous voice, Mills had labored tirelessly over the preceding weeks to commit Yale to a shutdown, addressing each of the residential colleges in turn with a calmly expressed sense of alarm that could be more hair-raising than the most inflammatory Panther rhetoric.

Mills was very conspicuous at the Rink meeting, attired in his customary workman's denim, hovering near the platform and planning strategies, as well as delivering one of the opening speeches. Mills was followed by graduate students, officials from the Hill community, a representative of a women's liberation group ("Women are an oppressed group at Yale") expressing solidarity with the oppressed Panthers, and the Reverend William Sloane Coffin. Here, to a moderately enthusiastic assembly, Coffin reaffirmed his dedication to non-violence and outlined his plan to submit himself, along with anyone else who cared to join, to mass arrest on the steps of the courthouse. (Coffin was later to cancel his march for fear of creating an uncontrollable situation). When he finished speaking, the chairman said, "I now return this meeting to the people."

The "people" dedicated themselves to pretty much the same themes: that it was impossible for black people to remain non-violent when they were being subjected to daily violence from police; that the Panther trial was a political trial; that if the trial was not called off, New Haven and Yale would have to suffer the flaming consequences. A number of muscular, glowering black men in leather jackets began to take up positions on the floor and along the aisles of the bleachers, standing with their arms folded while Charles Garry, the Panther Defense Counsel, introduced the principal speaker of the evening, Panther Chief of Staff David Hilliard. Hilliard entered the rink to tumultuous applause and a standing ovation. The students raised their clenched fists, shouting "Right On" and "Power to the People."

Hilliard took the platform, backed by four burly bodyguards in black berets, and waved his arms to the enthusiastic crowd. "There is a very basic decision facing racist America," he began, "as to whether we will allow this country to become openly fascist, or whether we will wage revolutionary struggle to bring order to the disorder of this country. When black men are snatched out of courtrooms and taken to prisons, then brought before judges and reprimanded as if we were criminals to apologize for wrongdoings that were meted out against us, then I see that somewhat as a compromise. But there are distinctions between revolutionary compromises and reactionary compromises.

That statement was necessary to allow us another day of freedom."

Hilliard paused. "But just because we were crafty enough to outwit the stupid demonic persecutors of black people in this country, we're going to take the opportunity to say *Fuck the judicial system!* Next time we're going to rot in jail rather than compromise. And that's my confession to Yale."

"We have a revolutionary brother in Berkeley," Hilliard continued. "The brother is charged with four counts of attempted murder of four pigs. And I don't think that's wrong. Because everybody knows that pigs are depraved traducers that violate the lives of human beings and that there ain't nothing wrong with taking the life of a motherfucking pig."

The cries of "Right on!" were now getting confused with some boos from the crowd which began to mount in volume as more of the audience absorbed what Hilliard had just said. "That's the best thing that happened here tonight," Hilliard continued. "Those boos. Because you give me room to tell you people my real feelings. . . . I knew you motherfuckers were racist. I didn't have any doubts."

The boos did not diminish in volume after this outburst, and this made Hilliard's anger blossom. "Boo me right on out of this motherfucker. Boo me right

back to Litchfield jail. Go boo me again, racists! . . .
Go on back to your humanities classes, go back to
your psychology classes, or your English 3 or whatever
it is." The booers paused for a moment, perhaps shaken
by Hilliard's accusations concerning their racial feelings and academic commitments.

"Because we know this is a real situation — because
we're suffering," Hilliard said, as the crowd grew quiet.
"We're dying in the streets, we're facing the threat of
torture in the electric chair, and I say Yale has a long
way to go if they don't think we're hostile and that
we're not angered by the inactivity of a bunch of
young stupid motherfuckers that boo me when I speak
about killing pigs. I say Fuck you!"

The boos had begun again, louder than ever. Hilliard
stared at the crowd stonily. "Boo. Boo. Boo," he began to join in. "Boo Ho Chi Minh. Boo the Koreans.
Boo the Latin Americans. Boo the Africans. Boo all
the suffering blacks in this country. You're a goddam
fool if you think I'm going to stand up here and let a
bunch of so-called pacifists, you violent motherfuckers,
boo me without me getting violent with you."

His tone was suddenly restrained. "Because," and
here he paused to let the audience absorb the full
liberterian impact of his words, "because I understand
that although you don't agree with what I have to

say, you should be intelligent enough to tolerate that other than boo me."

At this, the black students and faculty ranged in the bleachers behind the platform rose to their feet and applauded Hilliard; and this brought a number of white students to their feet as well. A more tolerant spirit began to fuse through the crowd, and Hilliard found it possible to smile once again. In this more friendly atmosphere, Hilliard reminded the crowd of the possibilities of race war, and of those who say it is inevitable in this country. "I think such a war might just be headed off," Hilliard said, "but that statement is supported when you all boo me."

As if reminding himself of his unpleasant reception, Hilliard began to warn the crowd: "If there's any assassinators in the audience, if there's anyone crazy enough to come up here and supplant that booing by sticking a dagger in my back or shooting me in the head with a . . . Magnum, then let's do that, because I know that will be the one spark that will set off the reaction that will civilize racists in this country and hopefully in the motherfucking world."

Hilliard paused for a little consultation with the strategists in front of the platform, none of whom looked happy at the turn of events. When he spoke again, his tone was milder and more humorous.

"Now you got me talking to you like a crazy nigger
— you got me talking like your mothers and fathers
talk to you. I've called you everything but longhaired
hippies. . . . And now I want to compound my sin by
calling you longhaired hippie Yale motherfuckers.
Fuck you."

The booing had stopped, but an air of puzzlement
permeated the crowd over whether Hilliard was putting
them on. Hilliard resolved this by holding out his
arms and saying, "Now I'm going to take it all back —
I take it all back, everything I said to you. On the
grounds that you repudiate your boos." The assembly
responded to this new revolutionary compromise with
deafening applause. Good-natured liberalism was
about to prevail after all. Hilliard began to shout into
the mike: Power to the People. POWER TO THE
PEOPLE. The crowd took up the chant, rising to its
feet and holding up clenched fists.

Now there was considerable activity erupting behind
and to the left of the speaker's platform. A young
white man in shirtsleeves was seen struggling with
Hilliard's bodyguards, and the black men stationed
around the rink started to move swiftly from their
positions. Suddenly, the white man was being struck
by the bodyguards. Soon he was down on the ground,
and the bodyguards were kicking and stomping on
him. Although this struggle was visible to those of us

in the bleachers, the crowd on the floor began to receive the information slowly, like a ripple of water
turning into a wave. The crowd began to shout in dismay, and Hilliard announced that a "reactionary"
had been prevented from taking over the platform.
The "reactionary" was now completely encircled by
blacks who continued to stomp on him, until Ken
Mills, aided by students, extricated the white man
and helped him stand up.

As the young man was being helped to his feet,
Hilliard told the shouting crowd: "I think that was a
humane response to all those who try to block the
legitimate struggle of black people in this country. I
think that anybody who takes the opportunity to
come up here and run me or any other individual off
the platform deserves that kind of treatment — and
if they don't want that, then keep their motherfucking
asses down."

Hilliard's remarks were, predictably, greeted with
boos, and Hilliard, predictably, returned to his refrain
about "the essence of democracy," toleration of different opinions. But the mood of the crowd had
changed. Hilliard was not going to win it back so
easily. After attempting some jocular remarks ("It's
lucky I wasn't smoking pot or dropping LSD because
I would have kicked his motherfucking ass too"),
Hilliard wisely decided to finish his speech and leave.

Collecting his bodyguards around him, Hilliard concluded by cursing Yale students for being fake revolutionaries ("You only want to be entertained") and shouting "All power to all those except those who want to act like motherfucking racists."

Ken Mills was now addressing the crowd in his calm, tired voice: "This meeting was called by the Moratorium Committee. We did not schedule it as a debate." The beaten white man (later identified as a student at the School of Architecture) was on the platform behind Mills, carefully taking notes off the speaker's lectern and throwing them on the floor. Cries of "Let him speak" rose from the floor. Mills responded: "Nevertheless . . . this particular gentleman may speak and after that we shall get back to the business for which this meeting was called."

The beaten man stood silently, with his head down. His shirt was torn and his face was dirty, but there were no signs of blood on his body. The crowd watched him with intent curiosity, as he allowed three minutes to pass in absolute silence. Then he began to pace up and down the platform, shaking his head. The audience was growing restive. A few students began to shout witticisms at the man.

Finally, after five minutes, the young man came up to the microphone and blew into it. The crowd applauded. Silence. He hit the mike a few times with his fingers and popped the loudspeakers. More jokes from the crowd. Now he began to scrape the lectern with his fingernails. It occurred to me that he was executing an extraordinarily clever piece of theatre: He would stand for a period of time, turning himself into a mute testimony, and then he would leave.

But then he spoke. He had a pronounced foreign accent. (Later I discovered that the student was a citizen of Lebanon, of Greek extraction). "A small step for mankind, a big step for me — whatever that implies or means or invokes. . . ."

More silence. "Louder," shouted a member of the audience. Many laughed. The young man spoke again, more incoherently. Then he said: "This is a privileged position I have at the moment. Of course I'm hopeful that I'm worthy."

A tall thin figure in owlish glasses materialized on the platform, placing a gentle hand on the man's shoulder and speaking into the mike. "I'm Ken Keniston. I'm a psychologist.[1] I think this fellow is in trouble."

"I'm not in trouble," the man replied. He stammered a little. "I think it is you who are in trouble. I think it is all of you."

------

[1] Kenneth Keniston, author of *The Young Radicals*, is Professor of Psychiatry and Director of Behavioral Sciences at Yale.

Keniston put his arm around the student: "I'm
going to ask all of you for the greatest understanding
and sympathy at this point — and silence and respect
— while we try to help this guy."

There was sympathetic applause from the crowd as
Keniston, with the aid of some students, helped the
man off the platform and out of the hall. The young
man was seen a short time later on the streets of New
Haven, walking alone and muttering to himself.[2]

When the platform was cleared, Ken Mills took it
over again. "It isn't easy to deal with a situation of this
kind," he said, "and it demands understanding and
patience. I hope at this point we can be calm and get
back to the business we are trying to deal with . . .
and that business of course for us here at Yale (my
voice is going) is a consideration of what we are going
to do about the defense of justice for the Panthers
and to retain whatever humanity we still have left. A

---

[2] I subsequently asked Professor Keniston if he knew what
had happened to this student. He told me that some days later
the student's friends had asked advice about how to help him;
Keniston suggested they call University Health. At this writing
(May, 1970), the student is in Bellevue, having been brought
there when he tried to enter an art museum forcibly after it had
closed, reportedly to look at a painting that reminded him of
home. Officials at the School of Architecture are trying to have
him transferred to Yale-New Haven Hospital.

condition such as the one we have just seen is a kind of condition that can befall any of us at any time in a society like this. It really is in that sense something we should think about quite deeply."

"Yale is now the target," Mills continued, "and the question now is how to prevent that kind of holocaust and destruction that in many ways nobody here wants and yet that arises out of the nature of conflict and injustice in our society. I call for an acclamation that shows you are serious, and that the shutdown is now."

At this point, a number of students took up the call of *Strike* and were joined by many, though by no means all, of the crowd. The students then left to attend late-night meetings at their individual colleges where nine of the twelve colleges voted to shut down academically, and to open up their facilities to out-of-town demonstrators on the weekend of May 1st. From that point on, the large majority of Yale students stayed away from class, some to attend teach-ins, some to discuss the issues with the residents of New Haven, some to train as marshals and hold down violence on the weekend. In this way, they hoped to express resistance to the Panther suppression and dismay over the legal system in America, to save Yale, and to demonstrate a sympathetic concern.

II

On the next day, we held a general meeting at the School of Drama to determine our own position vis-a-vis the strike. Although I was still teaching, as well as directing with the repertory company, I had been on leave from administrative duties during the spring term, and so I attended this meeting as a faculty member rather than as Dean. Acting Dean Howard Stein presided. The meeting was passionate and highly charged. Rumors had begun to accumulate about the kind of violence to be expected on May 1st weekend, and many of the students were fearful, as well as enraged, over the society that had brought things to this pass. Like the majority of students at Yale, the students of the Drama School were eager to prevent a major conflagration from occurring in New Haven, at the same time that they were looking for some way to express themselves actively concerning the condition of black people in this country. For this reason, our students were torn between shutting down operations altogether (the position of the radicals) and "redirecting" the school's activities (the position of the moderates) so that classes and productions might be more directly centered on America's political dilemmas. As the debate evolved, it became clear that a number of

new demands were getting tacked on the original strike
proposal, regarding not only the freeing of the New
Haven Panthers and the cancellation of the trial, but
the creation of a free Day Care center for the children
of employees at Yale; the termination of construction
on Route 34, which, it was said, would act as a barrier
between the black and white communities; the abolition of the proposed social science center on the
grounds that Yale social scientists treat blacks as experimental objects; the introduction of unemployment
compensation for all campus workers; and the establishment by Yale of a five million dollar fund for "the
immediate construction of 2000 units of low- and
moderate-income housing" in New Haven.

The black students of the school sat quietly, but
with obvious impatience, as the white radicals began
to append their own concerns to the matter at hand;
before the end of the meeting, most of them had left.
I was rather touched by the sense of omnipotence with
which students, both black and white, tended to invest the university — assuming that either Yale or
Kingman Brewster had the power to halt criminal proceedings, stop road construction, and solve the housing
problems of the New Haven community. I rose to
say at this meeting that, while I was contributing money
to a direct trust set up by John Hersey to pay the legal
fees of the Panthers, I was not convinced that the

aspirations and needs of the black community were identical with the aims of the Black Panthers. For those who wished to express solidarity with the Panthers rather than help assure that the trial be a fair one, I tried to remind the meeting that the Panthers were openly dedicated to the extermination of the "pigs" and a Maoist revolution with violent aims, and that their attitude towards Jews was openly hostile. I also felt compelled to say that somebody had committed a particularly brutal murder of a black man, that two of the defendants had already confessed to complicity in the crime, and that (no matter how discredited such testimony might later prove to be) this seemed sufficient grounds for a trial to take place. It was important, I thought, not to prejudge this trial, but rather to bend our energies to see that New Haven did not repeat the injustices done to the Panthers elsewhere in the country.[3]

The students voted not to shut down but rather to redirect the energies of the school indefinitely. Although this vote was not binding on the administration (governance at the School is still in the hands of its

---

[3] New Haven, it is commonly agreed, did not repeat these injustices. Thus far, the trials have been relatively fair, and the convictions have been largely based on guilty pleas and/or confessions.

faculty), Dean Stein agreed to a modification of the existing training, providing it was voluntary on the part of the instructors and students, and providing it took place within the existing class schedule. In this way, students who wished to study could still pursue their academic work, while the others had the option of staying away and functioning through direct political action or through their area of expertise, the theatre. Some students wanted to engage in guerilla theatre demonstrations on May 1st, others wished to reenact daily the trial's proceedings using the transcript as a text, still others went into training as marshals. One of our faculty and company members, Carmen de Lavallade, expressed her concern for the black high-school kids who were beginning to roam the city, many of them getting arrested for breaking windows and snatching pocketbooks; and she suggested that drama students bring rehearsed productions to Lee and Hillhouse High to keep the kids in school and off the streets. Inevitably put into question was the "relevance" of coming drama school productions, including the first- and second-year acting projects, and the production of Don Juan. But although a few students were anxious to convert all of our activity to political action, the great majority insisted on preserving the freedom of individuals to choose their own ways. The two student acting projects, in fact, continued to rehearse,

and many classes met with almost normal attendance
and continued to function in a quasi-academic manner, despite the increased activity of students in the
field.

I went from the school meeting to the theatre. Our
rehearsal had been delayed, as many of our rehearsals
would be delayed over the next week for crises and
meetings. I was anxious to meet with the company
and to hear its feelings and desires concerning the
strike, since what had just transpired at the school
was bound to affect our work. We worried together
over the possible risks of proceeding with the last few
performances of our current production (a trio of
plays by Yale writers called *Transformations*), assuming that a public display of business-as-usual was
bound to enrage Yale's more radical students. Despite
their personal fears, however, the company voted unanimously to proceed with the performances, as well as
with rehearsals of *Don Juan*. Actors continually agonize,
these days, over the unworthiness of their profession
and the unimportance of their function — but when
the chips are down, they show traditional courage and
dedication to their art.

One of the box office girls broke in at this point.
"Aren't you going to do *anything* to support the strike?"

"What do you suggest we do?" I answered.

"Close down the theatre," she said, "and give the

place over to some black groups. Or contribute the
receipts to the Panther Defense."

"Well, if we cancel our performances at the church
here, we'll have no way to pay salaries (I won't mention the breach with our audiences). You know, your
own salary comes through the box office receipts. If
you're willing to give up your paycheck this week, I'll
ask the others how they feel about it, so at least we
can be generous personally instead of institutionally."[4]

"That's not the question," she said. "I can't stand it
that the theatre is doing nothing at all about the
situation."

"Well, you have your options," I said.

She exercised one, and quit.

On the next day, I ended rehearsal early so I could
attend the Yale College faculty meeting. On my way
to Sprague Hall, I passed a crowd of students gathering at Beinecke Plaza. A mass meeting had been called
for that afternoon, which was to march to the steps
of Sprague while the faculty was in session in order to
impress on us the need for action. Graffiti had begun

---

[4] A black student group did apply for space to put on a production and was given the University Theatre, with its larger
seating capacity. As for the Repertory Theatre, we later received
permission from the university to donate our weekday box office
proceeds during the run of Don Juan to the Calvin Hill Day
Care Center for the children of employees of Yale.

to appear on the walls, fences, and gates of Yale, some
of it threatening (*Babylon will burn!*), some romantic
(*Z*), some epigrammatic (*Theft is the moral obligation
of the poor*), while huge STRIKE letters were being
painted in red everywhere.

Before the faculty meeting began, I was told an
interesting story. A distinguished professor of history
at Yale had walked up to some members of the Strike
Steering Committee and said in an excited voice:
"Have you heard the news? They found the body of a
man — dreadfully tortured, with manacles on his wrists
and cigarette burns on his testicles. And he was black!"
After their initial shock had given way to fury, the
students demanded to know where. "In Middlefield
swamp," replied the professor, and walked away. It was
one of the few references to Alex Rackley made during
those weeks.

Kingman Brewster had been scheduled to begin the
meeting with a statement, but he yielded the floor to
Professor Roy Bryce Laporte, chairman of the African
Studies program, who presented a resolution on behalf
of the black faculty at Yale. This asked the President
to issue a directive, calling — among other things — for
all members of the university to support an indefinite
suspension of normal academic functions in recognition
of the oppression of Panthers and blacks throughout
the land. The resolution was then tabled while Brew-

ster made his now famous remarks concerning his skepticism over "the ability of black revolutionaries to achieve a fair trial anywhere in the United States" as a result of "the atmosphere . . . created by police actions and prosecutions against the Panthers." It is worth emphasizing once again that Mr. Brewster's remarks were clearly offered as a personal opinion rather than an official policy, and so it remains remarkable that they could have generated so much indignation.

An alternate resolution was then submitted, sponsored by Kenneth Keniston, Peter Brooks, and Charles Long suggesting that the faculty have the option of holding their classes, cancelling them, or "redirecting" them toward the issues of the trial until after May 4th, the Tuesday after the May 1st weekend; this resolution also contained a clause asking the faculty to affirm once again that violence had no place on a university campus. It was clear that a majority of the faculty was eager to endorse some compromise between these two resolutions, and to endorse it quickly, since the shouts of students milling on the steps could now be heard. Dean Georges May, the presiding officer, announced that a representative of this crowd (estimated at more than a thousand students) had asked permission to address the faculty, and May suggested a suspension of the rules so that this representative might appear. The faculty agreed unanimously. Kurt Schmoke, a very

popular black member of the class of 1971, proceeded
to impress further on the faculty the desperate need
for fast support of the student position. When he left,
the entire faculty rose to its feet as an expression of
homage to the courtesy of his speech and the charm of
his person.

The debate that followed focused mainly on the two
points of difference between the black faculty resolution and the Keniston-Brooks-Long resolution — the
decision whether to have a complete shutdown or an
optional "redirection" of university activities, and the
duration of the suspension proposed. President Brewster, who was soon to call the question (thus effectually
shortening the debate), helped resolve the first difference by suggesting a rewording of the black faculty
motion in order to leave some margin of choice for
individual faculty members: The new wording directed
that the normal academic expectations (not functions)
of the university be modified (not suspended). This
committed us to "redirection," and to this the black
faculty cordially agreed. They also agreed to accept
an amendment to their resolution from Kenneth
Keniston, which included the clause from his resolution regarding non-violence. But when Keniston tried
to introduce another amendment establishing May 4th
as the date reestablishing normal university activities,
Kenneth Mills came over to his seat to tell him that were

he to insist on this, the black faculty would feel compelled to walk out of the meeting. After overhearing this, I took the opportunity to rise on a point of information, reminding the faculty that it was voting for an *indefinite* suspension of normal activities, and emphasizing that a clause affirming non-violent principles could have little force when the black faculty resolution proposed that no penalties be imposed for any actions performed during this period. Kenneth Mills replied to these objections by reminding the faculty it could always reconvene the university by meeting again after the May 1st weekend, and that the rules against violence and disruption would, of course, be expected to remain in effect. After this, the faculty voted overwhelmingly to endorse the amended black resolution.

I voted against, and left the meeting profoundly depressed.

Walking back to the theatre, I wondered at the alacrity with which a majority of the faculty could, in effect, vote away some of its academic freedom, considering the difficulty with which this freedom was gained in the first place. I am given to pessimism, and I began to foresee a time when the university could be shut down or "redirected" on the basis of any political crisis, thus making it impossible to proceed with the process of learning, teaching, creating, and research. I was amazed at the ease with which a group of intellec-

tuals, presumably devoted to their subjects, could suspend their right to teach, even for the briefest period.
Perhaps the students had managed to persuade large
numbers of faculty, after all, that what they were doing
was not really very important. The cry of "relevance"
that had been heard in the land over these years may
at last have gotten through to the academicians, and
the anti-intellectualism of our society was now beginning to triumph even in the home of the intellect.

And outside the home of the intellect? The Yale
faculty was under extraordinary pressure in making its
decision, but no such motive affected intellectuals in
the world at large. My friends include painters, writers,
film-makers, publishers, editors; with few exceptions,
they approved of Yale's decision to suspend its academic work during this period out of sympathy with
the Panther cause. Would my friend, the Action
painter, have changed his style to a realism more
compatible with depicting political injustice? Would
my friend, the film-maker, stop work on the youth
market movie he is making and begin one celebrating
the black revolution? Would my friend, the publisher,
halt production on all books that do not directly
examine the trials of the Panthers? Would my friend,
the novelist, "redirect" his next work into a nonfictional
documentary about the oppression of the blacks? Only
in the university is one expected to make his profes-

sional life identical with his political life, so that the
teaching of literature, history, philosophy, languages,
science, and art becomes something shameful whenever
the government commits another outrage.

A few days after the faculty meeting, a band of roving
students made what they called "a tour of the campus,"
stopping at libraries, the art museum, the Yale Daily
News, and the Repertory Theatre. They banged on our
doors, demanding to be admitted, and shouting, "Shut
it down!" We continued our work behind locked doors.

The next day, I was walking down York Street
behind a student I recognized; he was a dropout from
the Graduate Philosophy Department who had attempted unsuccessfully to revolutionize the Drama
School last spring. He turned around and, casting a
baleful eye on me, raised his fist and cried, "Power to
the people!" I nodded and walked on. Once again he
turned: "Power to the people!" I did not respond.
Then he stopped and faced me for a moment: "We're
going to give you something special this weekend to
write about in your articles. You're going to have plenty
of new material for The New York Times!" I thanked
him and asked, "Am I one of the people? Am I allowed
to have my say as well as you?" He turned silently, and
walked away with his raised fist clenched.

On Wednesday, the 29th of April, I was called away
from rehearsal by Dean Stein; he asked me to come to

his office immediately; my wife was there. When I arrived, I found her controlling herself with difficulty. She had just received a phone call at home. Somebody had asked, "Is Brustein there?" And when she offered to take a message, the voice said, 'Tell the pig he's going to die!' "

There was something ironic about this. Three years ago, we took our phone number out of the book, because right-wing patriots, aroused over my defense of a student workshop production in which a flag was used as a blanket, were making threatening calls. Now the left was on the phone, probably because I had recently written some articles satirizing revolutionary playacting and criticizing radical violence. The campus police informed me that a number of similar calls were being made to Yale faculty lately. I did not feel very comforted, especially when I learned that some birdshot had shattered my next-door neighbor's window the previous night. ("That shot was meant for me," I thought in my best paranoid fashion). I returned to rehearsal, after advising my wife to take herself and our six-year-old boy out of the house. I told the cast nothing, but arranged to hold rehearsals the next day in a space away from campus.

That night, my wife, my son, and I slept in Howard Johnson's Motor Lodge on Whitney Avenue, comparing its sanitized conveniences with the hiding places of our Jewish forebears. This made us decide to spend the next night home, so we left our child with a friend and returned to the house.

At a meeting with the deans, the President told us of the University's plans for the weekend: Yale was to remain open, and every effort would be made to offer hospitality to the visitors from out of town. In this way, he hoped to calm the fears of the Yale students and assure a peaceful weekend.[5] I advised him to close up the colleges and ask those students who had not already left New Haven to return to their homes. Rather than try to calm the students' growing apprehension, I said we were obliged to warn them in the strongest possible terms of the dangers that lay ahead that weekend. For the prospects were ominous. A large number of guns had been hijacked from various places; one fire had already been started in the Law School Library; a sizeable amount of mercury, which is used in homemade bombs, had been stolen from the

---

[5] In a letter to Yale parents and alumni, President Brewster explained his decision "to remain open during the May 1st weekend rather than to try to evacuate Yale or seal it off from New Haven during the rally sponsored by outsiders on the Green. Any shutdown or barricade, in my view, would immediately have provoked hostility and probably a violent test of strength. Worst of all, its clear contravention of freedom of speech and assembly would have radicalized otherwise moderate students."

chemistry lab; explosives had been discovered in the apartment of a Yale Weatherman dropout living in New Haven; and visits were expected from the most extreme elements on both the right and the left. I said that the decision to turn over college facilities to out-of-town demonstrators struck me as the height of folly. As a relevant cautionary tale, I outlined the plot of a play by Max Frisch called *Beidermann and the Firebugs*, where a guilty German businessman admits a number of arsonists into his home and, hoping to placate them, even provides the match with which they burn the place down. President Brewster, haggard and under obvious strain, had made his decision already and stuck to it. It was an extremely difficult decision, given his responsibility for the safety of Yale students, and I respected the difficulty with which he made it. I was immensely relieved when his strategy proved effective after all.

Thursday night, April 30th.

The black students of the school, together with some black undergraduates and young townspeople, put on a production called *Black Celebration* at the University Theatre. After this event, I meet at my home with Dwight Macdonald, Francine du Plessix Gray (covering the weekend for the *New York Review of Books*), Bill Coffin, and Dr. Robert Lifton, author and Professor of Psychiatry. Bill Coffin looks even more drawn than the President. He is off very soon for a late-night meeting with David Dellinger, hoping to persuade him to help keep the weekend cool. Coffin is very apprehensive over the potential for casualties during the next few days. I tell them the School of Drama has been closed for the weekend by order of Dean Stein, and I have called off rehearsals too; I will spend Friday and Saturday away from New Haven with my family, though within calling distance. I wonder aloud how many buildings will be burned or blown up that weekend and inquire why the Beinecke library has become such an object of student wrath. Bob Lifton asks me to understand why students would feel angry because so much money has been spent on a building for rare books, when so many problems in the country remain unsolved. I think about all the libraries and museums and wonder if their time is coming.

The weekend came and went without serious consequence. A bomb placed under the bleachers at Ingall's Rink, probably by a right-wing group, exploded shortly after most of the demonstrators had left a rock-and-roll concert there, resulting only in minor injuries. The buttery at Branford was burned and hacked with an axe by some of the visitors receiving hospitality there. Another fire was started in the Law School, and ten small fires were extinguished elsewhere on campus.

On the Green, a lot of angry rhetoric flowed, but the proceedings were relatively peaceful. In the most serious incident, the National Guard fired tear gas at a small group of enraged demonstrators marching on the courthouse after they had been misinformed by an unidentified black person that Panthers were being arrested by police. The Panthers had decided to cool the weekend and worked bravely and tirelessly for that purpose.[6] The Yale marshals, at risk of life and limb, helped to pacify the crowd. The New Haven police, under Police Chief James Ahern, acted in an admirably restrained manner. The black community kept the kids off the streets. And, I suppose, the National Guard troops, not to mention the four thousand federal troops stationed outside the city, helped to act as something of a deterrent.

Brewster's strategy had worked, and, miraculously, nobody had suffered serious injuries. Even the buildings, except for Ingall's Rink and some broken windows in the ROTC office, remained intact, though the graffiti had certainly accumulated. (Somebody tacked

---

[6] For the record, it should be noted that Panther policy considers the confrontation to be postponed rather than cancelled. On the Green, Douglas Miranda, New Haven Black Panther Captain, concluded his speech with these words: "All power to the people. And when the word is given, all power to the good shooters."

a sign on our theatre announcing, "The Drama School closed its doors on the revolution.") Then the awful events of Kent State and Cambodia exploded, mobilizing the campus to strike once again. But in spite of Ken Mills' efforts to keep the university shut down academically and opened up for political education during the summer, the President issued a directive reconvening classes — and a few students and faculty returned to regular duties. We even managed to open *Don Juan* on time, and some people even found it "relevant," in a somewhat broader than usual sense of that word.

So Yale got through its first rally for the Black Panthers. The trials began in July.

1970

5

The Crisis

of the

University

a. The Case for Professionalism

> In such state of society [a state of democratic anarchy], the master fears and flatters his scholars, and the scholars despise their masters and tutors; young and old are alike; and the young man is on a level with the old, and is ready to compete with him in word and deed; and old men condescend to the young and are full of pleasantry and gaiety; they are loth to be thought morose and authoritative, and therefore they adopt the manners of the young. . . .
>
> Plato, The Republic, Book VIII

Among the many valuable things on the verge of disintegration in contemporary America is the concept of professionalism — by which I mean to suggest a condition determined by training, experience, skill, and achievement (by remuneration, too, but this is secondary). In our intensely Romantic age, where so many activities are being politicized and objective judgments are continually colliding with subjective demands, the amateur is exalted as a kind of democratic culture hero, subject to no standards or restrictions. This development has been of concern to me because of its impact upon my immediate areas of interest — the theatre and theatre training — but its consequences can be seen everywhere, most conspicuously in the field of liberal

87

education. If the amateur is coequal — and some would
say, superior — to the professional, then the student
is coequal or superior to the professor, and "the young
man," as Plato puts it in his discourse on the conditions that lead to tyranny, "is on a level with the
old, and is ready to compete with him in word and
deed."

As recently as five years ago, this proposition would
have seemed remote; today, it has virtually become
established dogma, and its implementation is absorbing much of the energy of the young. Although student unrest was originally stimulated, and rightly so,
by such external issues as the war in Vietnam and the
social grievances of the blacks and the poor, it is now
more often aroused over internal issues of power and
influence in the university itself. Making an analogy
between democratic political systems and the university structure, students begin by demanding a representative voice in the "decisions that affect our lives,"
including questions of faculty tenure, curriculum
changes, grading, and academic discipline. As universities begin to grant some of these demands, thus tac-
itly accepting the analogy, the demands escalate to the
point where students are now insisting on a voice in
electing the university president, a role in choosing the
faculty, and even a place on the board of trustees.

I do not wish to comment here on the validity of

individual student demands — certainly, a student role
in university affairs is both practical and desirable, as
long as that role remains advisory. Nor will I take the
time to repeat the familiar litany of admiration for the
current student generation — it has, to my mind, already been sufficiently praised, even overpraised, since
for all its intrinsic passion, intelligence, and commitment, the proportion of serious, gifted, hard working
students remains about what it always was (if not actually dwindling for reasons I hope soon to develop).
I do want, however, to examine the analogy which is
now helping to politicize the university, and scholarship itself, because it seems to me full of falsehood.

Clearly, it is absurd to identify electoral with educational institutions. To compare the state with the
academy is to assume that the primary function of the
university is to govern and to rule. While the relationship between the administration and the faculty does
have certain political overtones, the faculty and administration can no more be considered the elected
representatives of the student body than the students
— who were admitted after voluntary application on
a selective and competitive basis — can be considered
freeborn citizens of a democratic state: The relationship
between teacher and student is mainly tutorial. Thus,
the faculty member functions not to represent the student's interests in relation to the administration, but

rather to communicate knowledge from one who knows to one who doesn't. That the reasoning behind this analogy has not been more frequently questioned indicates the extent to which some teachers are refusing to exercise their roles as professionals. During a time when all authority is being radically questioned, faculty members are becoming more and more reluctant to accept the responsibility of their wisdom and experience and are, therefore, often willing to abandon their authoritative position in order to placate the young.

The issue of authority is a crucial one here, and once again we can see how the concept of professionalism is being vitiated by false analogies. Because some authority is cruel, callow, or indifferent (notably the government in its treatment of certain urgent issues of the day), the Platonic idea of authority comes under attack. Because some faculty members are remote and pedantic, the credentials of distinguished scholars, artists, and intellectuals are ignored or rejected, and anyone taking charge of a classroom or a seminar is open to charges of "authoritarianism." This explains the hostility of many students toward the lecture course — where an "authority" communicates the fruits of his research, elaborating on unclear points when prodded by student questioning (still a valuable pedagogical technique, especially for beginning students, along with seminars and tutorials). Preferred to this, and therefore replacing it in some departments, is the discussion group or "rap session," where the student's opinion about the material receives more attention than the material itself, if indeed the material is still being treated. The idea — so central to scholarship — that there is an inherited body of knowledge to be transmitted from one generation to another — loses favor because it puts the student in an unacceptably subordinate position, with the result that the learning process gives way to a general free-for-all in which one man's opinion is as good as another's.

The problem is exacerbated in the humanities and social sciences with their more subjective criteria of judgment; one hardly senses the same difficulties in the clinical sciences. It is unlikely (though anything is possible these days) that medical students will insist on making a diagnosis through majority vote, or that students entering surgery will refuse anaesthesia because they want to participate in decisions that affect their lives and, therefore, demand to choose the surgeon's instruments or tell him where to cut. Obviously, some forms of authority are still respected, and some professionals remain untouched by the incursions of the amateur. In liberal education, however, where the development of the individual assumes such weight and importance, the subordination of mind to material is often looked on as some kind of repression. One begins to understand the current loss of interest in the past, which offers a literature and history verified to some extent by time, and the passionate concern with the immediate present, whose works still remain to be objectively evaluated. When one's educational concerns are contemporary, the material can be subordinated to one's own interests, whether political or aesthetic, as the contemporary literary journalist is often more occupied with his own ideas than with the book he reviews.

Allied to this problem, and compounding it, is the problem of the black students, who are sometimes inclined to reject the customary university curriculum as "irrelevant" to their interests, largely because of its orientation toward "white" culture and history. In its place, they demand courses dealing with the history and achievements of the black man, both in Africa and America. Wherever history or anthropology departments have failed to provide appropriate courses, this is a serious omission and should be rectified: Such an omission is an insult not only to black culture but to scholarship itself. But when black students begin clamoring for courses in black law, black business, black medicine, or black theatre, then the university is in danger of becoming the instrument of community hopes and aspirations rather than the repository of an already achieved culture. It is only one more step before the university is asked to serve propaganda purposes, usually of an activist nature: A recent course demanded by black law students at Yale, was to be called something like "white capitalist exploitation of the black ghetto poor."

On the one hand, the demand for "relevance" is an effort to make the university undertake the reparations that society should be paying. On the other, it is a form of solipsism, among both black students and white. And such solipsism is a serious threat to that "disinterestedness" that Matthew Arnold claimed to be the legitimate function of the scholar and the critic. The proper study of mankind becomes contemporary or future man; and the student focuses not on the outside world, past or present, so much as on a parochial corner of his own immediate needs. But this is childish, in addition to being Romantic, reflecting as it does the student's unwillingness to examine or conceive a world beyond the self. And here, the university seems to be paying a debt not of its own making — a debt incurred in the permissive home and the progressive school, where knowledge was usually of considerably less importance than self-expression.

In the schools, particularly, techniques of education always seemed to take precedence over the material to be communicated; lessons in democracy were frequently substituted for training in subjects; and everyone learned to be concerned citizens, often at the sacrifice of a solid education. I remember applying for a position many years ago in such a school. I was prepared to teach English literature, but was told no such subject was being offered. Instead, the students had a course called Core, which was meant to provide the essence of literature, history, civics, and the like. The students sat together at a round table to dramatize their essential equality with their instructor; the instructor — or rather, the coordinator, as he was called — remained completely unobtrusive; and instead of determining answers by investigation or the teacher's authority, they were decided upon by majority vote. I took my leave in haste, convinced that I was witnessing democracy totally misunderstood. That misunderstanding has invaded our institutions of higher learning.

For the scholastic habits of childhood and adolescence are now being extended into adulthood. The graduates of the Core course, and courses like it, are concentrating on the development of their "life-styles," chafing against restrictions of all kinds (words like "coercion" and "co-optation" are the current jargon), and demanding that all courses be geared to their personal requirements and individual interests. But this is not at all the function of the university. As Paul Goodman has observed, in The Community of Scholars, when you teach the child, you teach the person; when you teach the adolescent, you teach the subject through the person; *but when you teach the adult, you teach the subject.* Behind Goodman's observation lies the assumption that the university student is, or should already be, a developed personality, that he comes to the academy not to investigate his "life style" but to absorb what knowledge he can, and that he is, therefore, preparing himself, through study, research, and contemplation, to enter the community of professional scholars. In resisting this notion, some students reveal their desire to maintain the conditions of childhood, to preserve the liberty they enjoyed in their homes and secondary schools, to extend the privileges of a child- and youth-oriented culture into their mature years. They wish to remain amateurs.

One can see why Goodman has concluded that many of the university young do not deserve the name of students: They are creating conditions in which it is becoming virtually impossible to do intellectual work. In turning their political wrath from the social world, which is in serious need of reform (partly because of a breakdown in professionalism), to the academic world, which still has considerable value as a learning institution, they have determined, on the one hand, that society will remain as venal, as corrupt, as retrogressive as ever, and, on the other hand, that the university will no longer be able to proceed with the work of free inquiry for which it was founded. As an added irony, students, despite their professed distaste for the bureaucratic administration of the university, are now helping to construct — through the insane proliferation of student-faculty committees — a far vaster network of bureaucracy than ever before existed. This, added to their continual meetings, confrontations, and demonstrations — not to mention occupations and sit-ins — is leaving precious little time or energy either for their intellectual development, or for that of the faculty. As a result, attendance at classes has dropped drastically; exams are frequently skipped; and papers and reports are either late, under-researched, or permanently postponed. That the university needs improvement goes without saying. And students have been very helpful in breaking down its excesses of impersonality and attempting to sever its ties with the military-industrial complex. But students need improvement too, which they are hardly receiving through all this self-righteous bustle over power. That students should pay so much attention to this activity creates an even more serious problem: the specter of an ignorant, uninformed group of graduates or dropouts who (when they finally leave the academic sanctuary) are incompetent to deal with society's real evils or to function properly in professions they have chosen to enter.

It is often observed that the word *amateur* comes from the Latin verb, to love — presumably because the amateur is motivated by passion rather than money. Today's amateur, however, seems to love not his subject but himself. And his assault on authority — on the application of professional standards in judgment of his intellectual development — is a strategy to keep this self-love unalloyed. The permanent dream of this nation, a dream still to be realized, has been a dream of equal opportunity — the right of each man to discover wherein he might excel. But this is quite different from that sentimental egalitarianism which assumes that each man excels in everything. There is no blinking the fact that some people are brighter than others, some more beautiful, some more gifted. Any other conclusion is a degradation of the democratic dogma and promises a bleak future if universally insisted on — a future of monochromatic amateurism in which everybody has opinions, few have facts, nobody has an idea.

1969

b. The Decline of Professionalism

If the concept of professionalism is under assault today by the young, it is also being questioned by many professionals, both inside and outside the university. Here lies the greater threat to its existence. For a concept cannot really die until those who have traditionally preserved it through work and example begin to lose their beliefs, as now seems to be happening in our malfunctioning land. It is not just that the cult of amateurism is beginning to breach the walls of professionalism, but that the professionals are throwing over ladders and helping their assailants over the top. The children punish the parent; the patients analyze the doctor; the spectators push the actor off the stage; the students grade the teacher — all with the permission and encouragement of the older authority. The system of hierarchy — so infuriating to a democratic society, yet so essential to its survival — begins to break down, and men cannot hold firmly to their judgments, values, and standards.

One of the central sources of this collapse is the liberal faculty in the university. Sufficiently alert to incursions from external right wing threats to academic freedom, this faculty is virtually defenseless before the radical students within the gates. One reason is political, for liberalism is in crisis today. Filled with shame over a history that began with genocide and larceny — the extermination of the American Indian and the theft of his lands — and that now seems to be culminating in barbarous war, foreign adventures, racial inequality, domestic paralysis, economic collapse, perpetuation of poverty, and a gathering repression, the liberal faculty member shares the frustrations of the powerless at the same time that he enjoys the privileges of the elite. He pays the price of this dilemma in remorse, guilt, soul-searching, insecurity, and confusion. He begins to question the "relevance" of his own profession, and sometimes even the whole construct of Western civilization. Politically, he finds himself moving further and further toward the (new) left, which is to say, towards an area still unmarked except by indignation and innocence.

Psychologically, the liberal professor is left even more uncertain, for he is one of the more conspicuous victims of America's habit of worshipping youth. His profession puts him in daily contact with young people who perpetually besiege him with their life-styles — their special language, their colorful dress, their films, their music, all accentuated further by the mass media markets. Youth is everywhere, confident and vigorous and culturally approved, while he remains the fellow with the glasses and the educated speech, America's fall guy, doomed to reasonableness and prudence in a world of instinct, Oriental mysticism, blown minds, and casual promiscuity.

"Loth to be thought morose and authoritative," as Plato phrases it in the eighth book of *The Republic*, the "master," therefore, begins to "adopt the manners of the young." He lets his hair grow, first the sideburns, then the back; he exchanges his horn rims for granny glasses; he stops listening to classical albums and starts to dig the Rolling Stones and Steppenwolf; he begins to read extensively in Herman Hesse, Herbert Marcuse, Marshall MacLuhan, and R. D. Laing; he studs his speech with such phrases as "you know?" and "like — wow!"; he begins to talk a lot about "community," and joins the kids at pot parties and encounter sessions; he grows ecstatic over the callouses on the palms of student dropouts back from harvesting with the Venceremos Brigade in Cuba; he grows excessively solicitous of his non-white students; he sees the occupation of administration buildings as making the university a healthier place to be; and perhaps for the first time in his life, he begins to organize committees, sign petitions, and make ringing speeches at protest meetings.

"The master fears and flatters his scholars . . . and the young man is on a level with the old . . . and old men condescend to the young and are full of pleasantry and gaiety," writes Plato, who may have known something of the liberal teacher's pressing need to have the approval of his students, to be popular and well-liked. This kind of flattery is taking many forms, one of them being increasing experimentation with the university curriculum. Teachers trained in one professional discipline are beginning more and more to respond to student pressure for special "relevant" courses outside their area of expertise (magic, astrology, rock music, mysticism, racism, etc.). And while some of these new courses are useful and even necessary, most are merely extensions of current vogues and fashions, substantiated neither by ideas nor scholarship. The rationale for the new courses is that both teacher and students are being "educated" together in the immediate interests of the day, but, in actuality, only the teacher is being "educated," since the students have usually explored these enthusiasms already.

From one point of view, this curriculum revision is only a harmless waste of time; from another, it is threatening to have serious consequences for genuine scholarship. For the traditional subjects, whose "relevance" may not be immediately apparent to most students, are losing that discipleship that enables them to survive. The university ceases to be a conservatory of knowledge, to be reinterpreted and expanded by master and scholar as a result of new discoveries, and becomes instead a base for improvisation, where interest in a subject lasts only as long as the fashion. If one of the basic tests of a civilization (in Richard Lowenthal's words) is "the ability to transmit to the young generation its essential values while adapting their concrete, practical meaning to changing conditions," then clearly the American civilization is failing, partly through the progressive enfeeblement of the liberal faculty's faith and will.

Undermining this faculty's confidence in its function even further is a pernicious utilitarianism, which has now been transferred wholesale from America's heartland to the heart of the university. As Theodore J. Lowi has observed, the new student movements now share with "the respectable elements of the community" a "basic antagonism to theory, a deeply anti-intellectual impatience with academic efforts to distort reality by imposing a logical order on it. . . . It is a grand American tradition to hallow the immediate utility of knowledge."[1] In the past, this "grand Amer-

---

[1] "Yesterday's Revolutionists: The Faculty and the Tragedy of the University," *Midway* (Winter 1970). Compare the conclusions of Kenneth Keniston, in his article "Youth, Change and Violence" (1969): "Among post-modern youth, one finds a virtually unanimous rejection of the 'merely academic.' . . . It would be wrong simply to label this trend 'anti-intellectual,' for many new radicals and not a few hippies are themselves highly intellectual people. What is demanded is that intelligence should be engaged with the world, just as action should be informed by knowledge." As Professor Lowi would tell us, this is precisely what is meant by "anti-intellectual."

ican tradition" was responsible for a generalized contempt for disinterested speculation and scholarly research ("Basic research," said Eisenhower's Secretary of Defense, Charles Wilson, "is science's attempt to prove that grass is green"); today, it has invaded the academy itself where the value of the life of the mind is generally unperceived by most students in their demand for purely service functions for the university. Like the American businessman, who could find no way to justify learning, culture, or art unless they provided an immediately recognizable practical utility, the American student is declaring "irrelevant" anything that does not instantly lead to social progress and political change. Sensible enough to criticize the university for its collaboration with industry, government, and the military, the American student responds not by demanding a return to traditional academic aloofness and autonomy but rather by trying to make the university conform to the immediate needs of the surrounding civic community.[2]

---

[2] Professor Lowi observes: "Administrators are continually finding it necessary to justify the university in terms of the services it renders, the 'community resources' to be found there, the problem-solving capacities to be found there. . . . The militants get tremendous support from the central mass of students when they cry out against the institutional racism of a university encouraging Greek and teaching functionalist theory in social science 'when people out there are starving.' "

What is more, he is succeeding, and the liberal faculty is helping him. The shouts of "relevance" that have been cracking our ears for the past half decade are now reverberating through the halls of almost every university department, and particularly through the corridors of the social sciences. The rapid rise in power, popularity, and enrollment of these disciplines over the last few years can, I think, be attributed directly to the fact that they are so easily acceptable as a "relevant" course of study — especially when, as in the case of sociology and social psychology, they can be enlisted in the cause of improving society. This quasi-activist role for the social sciences is relatively new, which may explain why it is still, to some extent, disguised. But the capacity of these disciplines to be at the same time service-oriented (or "social") and academic (or "scientific") makes them perfect candidates for providing a utilitarian bridge between the university and the community.

The social claim of the social sciences is valid enough; what is harder to validate is their scientific claim. The problem with any discipline that tries to be both investigative and progressive is that the balance is so hard to maintain: One's sympathies are not always confirmed by one's research. The great temptation of the social scientist (successfully resisted, of course, by the really brilliant and original practitioners in the

field) is to weight the evidence in favor of his prejudices, thereby smuggling in advocate feelings under a
pretext of impartiality. I admit this may seem a strange
complaint coming from one like myself who (along
with a number of other literary and political intellectuals in the fifties) used to criticize the social scientist
for his dry, colorless style, and his substitution of statistics, polls, interviews, and charts for straightforward
judgments of taste and behavior. But it is really the
same complaint. For the point we were trying to make
about the sociologist of the fifties was that by lavishing
so much attention on mass culture, and by examining
motives and causes rather than actions and results, he
often seemed to be elevating cheap art into a position
of eminence, using analytical techniques to justify debased popular tastes. "When you begin to ask 'What
is it?' " as I wrote in "The Madison Avenue Villain"
(1961), "instead of 'Is it good?' you are already on
your way to joining 'it'."

Today, the concerns of the social scientist are different, but his temptations remain the same — manipulating scientific research to support ideological presuppositions. Contemporary social studies are often concerned with the very student generation that is enrolling
in them, with the nice result that the student may end
up studying himself. Innumerable works in the field
are now being published analyzing the committed and

the uncommitted, protean man and liberated woman,
young radicals and college dropouts, the New Left and
the hippies. And once again, we find the social scientist on his way to joining "it"; for, under the guise of
dispassionate investigation, he is more often than not
extolling youthful politics, attitudes, and life-styles.[3]
(The most skeptical critics of the radical young — as
of mass culture in the past — are still the radical hu-
manist intellectuals, along with certain tough-minded
liberal sociologists like David Riesman.) Thus, an entire field of academic study can begin to be dominated
by those who would adopt and glorify the manners of
the young.

By providing such services, the social sciences are
opening up the university for politicization, since it is
only natural, in a time of crisis, that the analysts of

---

[3] In *The Young Radicals* (1968), Keniston mentions "the
frequent feeling of many who have worked intensively with
today's dissenting youth that, apart from the 'impracticality' of
some of their views, these sometimes seem to be the only clear-
eyed and sane people in a society and a world where most of
us are systematically blind to the traditional gap between personal principle and practice, national creed and policy." Elsewhere, he writes: "These young radicals are unusual in their
sensitivity to violence, as in their need and ability to oppose it."
Recently Keniston has seemed more willing to concede that
young radicals may have aggressive tendencies like everyone else,
and his later articles make some effort to explain away such phe-
nomena as the Weatherman faction of SDS.

society should feel compelled to help change society actively. This seems to me an entirely honorable and important thing for individuals to do; but I am unalterable in my conviction that it is nothing for the university as a whole to do. Lest I be misunderstood, let me quickly affirm that university professionals have an obligation to make political choices (even if their choice is to be indifferent to politics), but it is just as obligatory for them to keep their professional and political lives distinct. The rock on which the university is founded is the search for truth, not the implementation of ideology, because without the truth — in all its quirky, idiosyncratic, maddening complexity — no ideology has a chance of survival, unless it is enforced through totalitarian methods. To import any orthodoxy wholesale into the university, and to modify or obscure the truth in order to suit the needs of an ideology, is to create a scandal of such magnitude that no university will long outlive it.

I am really arguing for the preservation of the *private* side of university professionalism (research, scholarship, laboratory experiment) which, like the private side of men, is not so easily adapted to social and political purposes. This seems an odd argument to be forced to make, considering that the university has always somehow managed, in a bustling world, to function as a haven of quiet reflection and peaceful contemplation. But now that the hostility Americans have traditionally felt for genuine academic pursuits has entered the university itself, students have proved very successful in persuading teachers that anything other than teaching and counseling is somehow selfish, anti-social, and "irrelevant." This is further reflected in the incredible demands now being made on the teacher's research time by students anxious for personal advice, attention, or simple companionship. And it is implied in their demand that "good teaching" compensate for lack of publication or contributions to the field, and that tenure be awarded on the basis of political correctness or work in the community. One can hardly fault the sentiments behind these demands, but they are hardly likely to improve the quality of university education. If the teacher does not have the time or encouragement for original thinking, he will have little of value to contribute to his class (and, by extension, to society as a whole). And he will be tempted into role-playing and spellbinding, entertainment at the cost of communication, and the development of the kind of style now so frequently seen at protest meetings and rallies.

These protest meetings and rallies, now becoming more and more a fixture of university life, are sufficient forewarnings of what is in store for us when academic affairs become politicized; for they have

grown increasingly authoritarian, uncivil, and monolithic in their tone. It is just a little harrowing to
watch "the only clear-eyed and sane people" in society
being manipulated like puppets by clever political
harangues, and, when their passions are aroused by
oratory, rising to their feet, waving clenched fists, and
shouting "Power to the people," as if they had just
stepped off a page of German history. In such an atmosphere, anyone who dares to offer an opposing point
of view must be very eccentric indeed, since the tolerance for dissent (I mean the *real* kind, not the conformist herd variety professed today) is extremely low.
When the university votes as a whole to address itself
entirely to a single issue, or to abandon its neutrality
as an institution and take some political position, then
the margin of academic freedom begins to narrow to
invisibility. Continuing to teach one's subject becomes
a betrayal of the democratic consensus, and any di-
vergence from a unified stand is identified as an effort
to "polarize" the community — as if the university had
a more important mission than to harbor different
opinions and attitudes, as if it could be "democratic"
in any sense other than its capacity to tolerate disagreement.

What is invidious about these protest meetings —
not to mention all the teach-ins, teach-outs, rap sessions, and other extra-academic innovations of our time

— is the common assumption that these are more important forms of "education" than what is gained in classrooms and libraries. And, indeed, when social responsibility rather than learning becomes the primary goal of academic life, then virtually anything can be justified in the name of "education." During the May Day events at Yale, some of the radical faculty wanted to "shut the university down so as to open it up to reality," while a number of liberal faculty members, including some high administration, expressed their conviction that students were being better "educated" by discussing the issues of the Black Panther trial than they could ever be in formal classes. These presumptions, so profoundly anti-intellectual and so arrogant in their concept of what constitutes "reality," are a direct consequence of our "relevance" madness, and another wound in the side of professionalism.

The problem lies in the loose way we use language, for, in such a context, the word *education* loses most of its meaning. It becomes related to that sentimental notion that all of life is an education, and that the best preparation for living is the "school of hard knocks." It is connected to the adage that "experience is the best teacher" (better than whom? Freud? Marx? Aristotle? Lorenz?), and that anything is to be preferred to mental discipline and intellectual training. It is a heritage of that shallow and misunderstood Deweyism

that has been taught for years in teachers' colleges,
and that has hitherto been reserved for students below
the university level. It is the shared assumption of
students who have no interest in the life of the mind
or curiosity about history, and of liberal faculty too
embarrassed about their "useless" function in a time
of stress to remember why they entered the intellectual life in the first place.

I do not wish to be insensitive to the national crisis
in trying to defend the sanctuary of the private university. I share great anguish about our failures as a
nation and fully understand why many would prefer
the university to be a service institution rather than
a professional academy. When a national administration refuses to confront the social and political imperatives of our time, one inevitably turns to more
accessible institutions for the redress of grievances, and
the university is clearly an infinitely more benevolent
agency than the government. Then, again, when a
government remains invulnerable to protest, the university, through a process of transfer, can be blamed
for the low quality of national life, and, even though
it lacks responsibility for our problems, can be made
to suffer institutionally as a surrogate.

What I would suggest, as a way of satisfying those
unhappy with the present academic structure, is a
parallel institution with purely service functions, situ-

ated right in the urban center. This might be called a "community college," in the sense that it would be a college for the use of the community, offering its neighbors in the area the services of mental health centers, social institutes, political organizing, urban planning, and radical theatre. Its faculty and student body would be made up of those presently convinced that traditional learning and research are obscene in a time like this and who wish to work directly on ghetto problems and ways to end the war. Its funds could be supplied by the city and by private donors, and by the levying of a graduated income tax on all its members, the more affluent radical students, of course, contributing a large share of that patrimony that they normally spend on automobiles, drugs, movies, and records. In this way, moral indignation could be joined to positive action, self-righteousness could be earned by real sacrifice, and "relevance" could develop a firmer meaning than its current use as a shield for the destruction of academic values and institutions.

In this way, too, the private university could be preserved as a place of learning, a conservatory of knowledge, and an academy for those devoted to the critical function. For without the development of learning, knowledge, and criticism, the way of action will be obscured. In an America dominated by violence, utilitarianism, anti-intellectualism, philistinism, youth worship, role-playing, and ideological lying, there must remain at least one institution where these qualities do not dominate. There must be one place left that is *conservative*, in the sense that it conserves what is valuable in our tradition; *liberal*, in its openness to dissenting points of view; *radical*, in its examination of the roots of our metaphysical, psychological, social, and political dilemmas; all of these in its determination to extend the privileges of higher education to everyone qualified by temperament, dedication, skill, and intelligence to enjoy them. There must exist one institution where men can invent on the basis of what is already known, and where experiment will be cherished for other than its practical application. In short, we must preserve one institution, in our mediocre and brutal culture, where excellence prevails, where professionalism is perpetuated, and where the works of civilization continue to be honored and esteemed.

1970

6

Appendices

a. A Reply to Eric Bentley

In May, 1969, my former colleague at Columbia, Eric Bentley, wrote a letter to The New Republic criticizing "The Case for Professionalism." Although he agreed with many of the conclusions in that article, he was disturbed by my lack of enthusiasm for the position of the radical young, and wondered aloud if I was not "going over to the enemy" as a result of having become a Dean. "Can American education be reconstructed without going outside existing academic politics?" he asked, going on to suggest that the sit-in or occupation be recognized as a legitimate form of protest, similar to strikes in labor-management disputes. He was particularly disturbed by my phrase regarding "the many valuable things on the verge of disintegration in contemporary America," and called this "pure conservatism." He concluded: "I would maintain that to abandon political radicalism in order to combat educational amateurism would be to empty out the baby with the bath." My reply follows:

My friend Eric Bentley has responded to what was intended to be an impersonal analysis of the eroding effect of student radicalism on the function of education with an argument which forces me into personal testimony and defense. Such is the intensity of today's quarrels, as he suggests himself, that old friends are pressed into public confrontations.

To Mr. Bentley's assertions that I am "going over to the enemy" or abandoning "political radicalism" or engaging in "defensive conservatism," I must reply

117

that I remain the man I always was — this may, indeed, be the source of our disagreement. As long ago
as the fifties, when Eric Bentley was sniffing out
"pseudo-radicalism" in American plays and productions (pace "The Missing Communist" and elsewhere), my major concern was with the defense of
free artistic expression, and the alteration of any institutions that inhibited or blocked this expression
(pace my "Madison Avenue Villain" and elsewhere).
I am not by nature an ideological animal. I was originally attracted to scholarship through a love of art,
and a respect for those men who were capable of
speaking the truth, even when it was awful or un-
fashionable. The substance of my writings (and the
theme of The Theatre of Revolt, as anyone knows
who has read past the title) concerns the doubleness
of great drama and the complexity of life, and so I
have always felt a revulsion from monolithic thinking
from any quarter.

Therefore, I do not love political radicalism for its
own sake, and I deplore the kind of thinking that ex-
presses itself in terms of "enemies" and "sides." Since
I was only a child in the thirties, I have no vestigial
nostalgia for the conflicts of that period; since I was
not particularly political in college, I do not feel compelled to relive my student radicalism today. In consequence, I do not share the current reflexive assumption

that radical movements are necessarily more humane
or more compassionate than other movements. I
hear the SDS affirm this, but I see no evidence in
fact. When I hear of a Columbia history professor having his arms pinioned by students about to occupy a
building and being hit in the face with a club, or of
the gentle lady president of Radcliffe being terrorized
by students protesting a minor disciplinary action, I
do not automatically think of the courteous Marxism
espoused by Brecht, but rather of the bully tactics used
by the Nazis (before they came to power) against the
educational institutions of another corrupt liberal regime, the Weimar Republic. (Yes, the police use these
tactics, too, when pulling out students — and should be
banned from the campus for the same reason.) The
SDS, and its supporters, always emphasizes its idealism when defending such actions; but I imagine National Socialism had idealists too (it was, after all, a
partially *socialist* movement). Anyway, as a student
of Ibsen and Shaw, Eric Bentley should be a little
more skeptical of actions taken under the name of
"idealism."

I loathe the Vietnam war, and I continue to support
the Resist movement in its efforts to end that war. My
question is whether the assault on the universities is
helping to end the war — or to deflect the nation's attention from it. With university news getting such

prominence these days in the media, the atrocities in Vietnam get elbowed off the front page, and so does the attention of the legislators who begin to pour their energies into making laws against disruption. It is obvious that the ROTC is an extension of the military on the campus, and I personally believe that it has no place whatsoever in the university, but I sincerely wonder how important this issue is in the order of priorities. While the great ROTC controversy of 1969 occupies the campus activists at Yale (and elsewhere), the Olin Mathiessen plant (and others) just down the street continues to pour out armaments that will be sent to Vietnam.

Of course the university has been impure in its relations with the government; of course its expansion into slum communities has left many homeless; of course many professors have been mentally isolated from the vital concerns of the day. And these are issues that require varying degrees of radical reform. But it is also true that the university has been at the center of Vietnam resistance, that it has been in the forefront of enlarging educational possibilities for all the people of the nation, and that it has been attracting (until recently) some of the best and most effective minds in the country. To concentrate on the purification of the universities to the exclusion of concluding the war and solving urban problems is to play

right into the hands of those who would perpetuate
the conflict and maintain the ghettos. If I had an SDS-
type mind, I would begin to suspect a conspiracy between the radical students and the Pentagon. As it is,
I will satisfy myself with psychological rather than
political explanations. The assault on the universities
sometimes looks less to me like honest idealism than
a grownup version of the bully game called "get the
guy with the glasses." (I notice one of my correspon-
dents offering to use a club against any lecturer he
found engaged in military research. One of the studies that should be conducted by students and faculty
alike is to what extent American violence has bruta-
lized people on all sides of the political spectrum.)

My article was an implicit demand on people not to
polarize dumbly into unthinking positions, but to keep
alert to brutality wherever it may appear. In some non-
polemical, nonpolitical corner of his mind, Eric Bentley must have realized that the "valuable things on
the verge of disintegration" I referred to were not the
social or political institutions that he (and I) may find
wanting, but rather the kinds of conditions that were
able to produce a Faulkner, a Fitzgerald, a Heming-
way, an O'Neill, an Eliot, a Robert Lowell, an Ed-
mund Wilson, a Lionel Trilling — in other words, the
various consolations provided by art and intellect that
are now in danger of being obliterated by clenched

fists and clenched minds. The kind of thinking and writing being inspired by our current situation frankly appalls me: I do not think it is inapposite to observe how few legitimate works of art and intellect have been produced by the radical young, for all the ferment of the past three years (admittedly, I do not count rock music). I seem to remember that the French Revolution wasn't very impressive in its cultural achievements either, apart from Delacroix — and man cannot live on revolution alone.

He cannot live on "relevance" alone either. My very simple point was that in order to become a doctor and help the sick of the ghettos, you must first study "irrelevant" subjects like comparative anatomy and organic chemistry. In the same way, you must give yourself up to the seeming irrelevancies of the past in order to be relevant to the present. Otherwise, you will be condemned to repeat the errors of history, as the saying goes — and as we seem to be doing at the present moment. Clearly, the system is not working, and I share a profound sense of disturbance about it. But I do not believe it can or should be improved by violence, and the eagerness of the radical young to escalate their actions to their irrational rhetoric makes me worry whether the society they would substitute would not be worse than the one we now have. What we need are ideas, not romantic gestures, and the current situation is preventing ideas from being formulated.

A last word. I must be very careful — indeed, everyone must be careful — not to generalize wildly about students. They are an incredibly diverse and various group of people. My quarrel is with radical students of the SDS persuasion; all others I can reason with. I believe in students, as must surely be obvious from the fact that I am continuing in my present academic post. The temptation these days to withdraw from the academy into private life is simply overwhelming; if I am not mistaken, Eric Bentley has yielded to this temptation himself (let us hope temporarily). But I still believe that the dialogue we are conducting can best be held *inside* the university — so long as that institution is permitted to function and survive.

Robert Brustein

b. Letters on "Revolution as Theatre"

These letters, along with my reply, appeared after the publication of "Revolution as Theatre" in the New Republic.

Sirs:

> "Take the people out of the theatre and put them
> in the streets: Poor reality! They forsake their Lord
> God in favor of his bad copyist!" — Georg Büch-
> ner, Danton's Death

The speaker in the play quoted above was in real life
an unemployed actor who organized, together with a
playwright, a theatre-boycott in 1789 that had enough
people on the streets inside of two days to storm the
Bastille. The Paris Communards of 1871 reformed the
organization of the theatre in recognition of the role
played by conventional, institutional theatre in suppressing the proletariat. . . . Considering the apparent
success of conventional theatre in suppressing revolutionary inclinations it is hardly surprising if those
who have had quite enough of the status quo should
reach for the unconventional forms of theatre to change

things. Street-corner theatre was used with considerable success during the student-worker revolt of May,
'68 in Paris as a means of political education.

To my way of thinking, no apologies need be made
for revolutionary drama acted out in the streets and
before the television cameras; the improvised drama
of invective has always been an alternative to violence.
Abbie Hoffman has expressed the revolutionary's choice
of effective action as being between comedy and martyr-
dom — and to get back into academic perspective, Aristotle does say that the Old Comedy originated with
improvised, invective dramas. Similar dramas are used
to this day among the Eskimos, for instance, as a means
of settling interpersonal disputes which might otherwise result in ambush. . . .

Provocation is intended to involve others (it may be
one of the few remaining avenues, in this jaded age,
of making contact with others); it may elicit open
sympathy and aid from those who before were merely
inclined to be sympathetic, and those who are un-
sympathetic or even antipathetic it may incite to acts
discrediting to themselves, which in turn will elicit
sympathy from the onlooker. And dress is — yes, including "Pancho Villa moustaches and granny glasses,
long hair" and all — dress is a dramatic device. (Abbie
Hoffman: "Long hair is just another prop.")

It is that "selfish white working class" to which Brustein refers whose spirits are in direct need of spiritual revolution; and it is again these people who do not pay their admission into the "moral institution" of the theatre. The revolution has to be brought literally home to them. The revolutionary show has to go into the streets where everyone can see it, must see it, nolens volens, and force itself to the attention of the great unwashed public — even at the cost of appearing comical or outlandish — if it is to have any hope of success. The same Schiller who pleaded for the "stage as a moral institution" argued in another essay, "On the Use of the Chorus in Tragedy":

> The palace of the kings is now closed, the courts have withdrawn indoors from the gates of the cities . . . the poet must open up the palaces again, he must lead the courts out under the open sky, he must restore all the immediacy of life that has been vitiated by artificial institutions.

That is the true mandate of idealism. Its aims will not be accomplished by pious wishing. Power to the people!

Gareth S. Penn
Berkeley, California

Sirs:

Dean Brustein would have young radicals lower their voices and settle down to a "revolution of the spirit." Far more romantically naive than any young revolutionary, he urges a rather nebulous "act of moral transcending, humane intelligence, and deliberate will." Over 40,000 of this generation are dead, hundreds of thousands more are maimed, jailed, or in exile. Yet Brustein urges us to be kind, warm, and decent. In an indecent world where our lives are on the line such a plea is folly or worse. Thus far violence on the part of this generation has been minimal. The theatrics and the demonstrations Brustein berates are in part the result of a desire to get change without violence. But instead of recognizing the commitment implied in the theatrics, Brustein sneers. His disgust can only intensify our despair. If the older generation chooses to sneer with him, the theatrics will inevitably give way to terrorism, and the battle Dean Brustein fears will be joined.

Charles M. Kerr
Stanford, Calif.

Sirs:

We of the New Left stage our drama for the same
reasons other playwrights do: to yield a meaning
through symbolic and dramatic representation. I assume that Mr. Brustein as critic can see beyond the
dialogue and costumes in the plays he reviews; why,
then, can't he see what's at the heart of the New Left
drama? . . . He seems to be asking us to prove we are
true revolutionaries by going wholly underground with
our ideology until we are ready to sabotage the President or bring off a military coup or something. That
is not our revolution, Mr. Brustein! We are the New
Left, the place is here, the time is now.

> *Annette Weatherman*
> *St. Louis, Mo.*

Robert Brustein replies:

1) In reply to Mr. Penn. My major objection to revolutionary theatrics as a conscious tactic of political indoctrination is that, so far, the scripts have been thin and the acting lousy. I am, moreover, skeptical about the radical theatre's power to affect anybody except those who are already converted (Andrew Sarris reports, for example, that Southern audiences give standing ovations to the rednecks of *Easy Rider* when they shoot the nonconformist bikers). What the theatre can do well under the best conditions is purge and enlighten — but for this you need great dramatists, not hysterics. The poet that Schiller refers to in Mr. Penn's quotation is presumably inspired; Abbie Hoffman is merely turned on.

Anyway, my original intention was not to argue about the effectiveness of political theatre, but rather to demonstrate — through the device of irony — how many of today's "revolutionaries" are playacting without knowing it. I do not think any significant change is ever going to come about in America until we can develop a much greater sense of reality, a quality admittedly in short supply in our sentimental times (so apparently is the capacity to comprehend irony). But a strong sense of reality is hardly compatible with the histrionic "revolutionary" temperament.

2) In reply to my other critics. Some time ago, five "revolutionary" students shot a sailor through the head in retaliation for the death of another student in an anti-ROTC demonstration, even though the sailor was not present at the site of the original killing and was unknown to his murderers. Was this action any different from the retaliatory killing of civilians by American soldiers in Vietnam? More recently, three young people blew themselves up on W. 11th St. with bombs said to be intended for Columbia University: Would these bombs, had they found their victims, have been different in kind from the police bullets that entered the body of Fred Hampton? The atrocities being prepared by Americans in the name of "revolutionary idealism" are very similar to the atrocities committed by Americans in the name of "defending the free world," even though the former have no official sanction and thus far (because of blunder) have caused no major catastrophe.* The one thing that unites Americans today on the left and right is indifference to the importance of human life. Perhaps somebody will tell

-----

* This was written before the bombing of the Army-Math building at the University of Wisconsin and the killing of a young graduate student there — also before the recent spate of murders of policemen.

me how one can condemn police brutality and military violence while adopting the same tactics.

I believe we must solve our problems by non-violent parliamentary means, regardless of the difficulties. There simply is no other way. If reform is blocked off at present, then the channels of reform must be opened again through imaginative programs, electoral pressures, endless nagging — any means short of violence. But this means creating a race that can understand, and this, in turn, means changes, internal and external, in the lives of us all. Since information and analysis are so essential to this process, perhaps all those social scientists who, just a few months past, were extolling the humane qualities of the New Left, would now tell us, please, a little more about the psychological makeup of America's young radicals.

c. Exchanges with Kenneth Keniston on "When the Panther Came to Yale"

After the appearance of "When the Panther Came to Yale," Professor Kenneth Keniston wrote a letter to the New York Times which published it along with my reply. Another letter from Professor Keniston, addressed to me with a copy to the Times, followed. Both of his letters are reprinted with his permission.

N. Y. Times Magazine, July 12, 1970,
To The Editor

I was shocked that my friend, Dean of the Drama School Robert Brustein, was threatened by an anonymous phone call before May Day. And it was only prudent for him to leave New Haven in the face of this intimidation. It is therefore quite understandable that Dean Brustein's personal recollections of the two weeks before May Day at Yale ("When The Panther Came To Yale," June 21) are dominated by images of intimidation, followed by injury or capitulation.

But the impact of this personal outrage has led Dean Brustein to dramatize the reaction of Yale as a whole in imagery that largely mirrors his own experience. In his portrait, each scene involves a glowering threat followed by terrory, injury, or surrender. Indeed, the only sane actor who appears on the stage is Dean Brustein, his lonely voice pleading for restraint, courage, and tolerance in a frantic and terrorized world. At a Drama School meeting, it was Dean Brustein who "tried to remind the meeting" of the real beliefs of the Panthers, and who "also felt compelled to say" that a murder had been committed. In the Yale College faculty meeting, the only uncompromised voice we hear is Dean Brustein's: after "overhearing" a threat, it was he who took "the opportunity to rise on a point of information, reminding the faculty . . . etc." And so on.

All this is excellent theatre — recurring scenes of intimidating revolutionaries and a terrorized community, punctuated only by a solitary, unheeded voice calling for reason. But it is poor history.

For example, approximately a third of his account is devoted to one meeting in Ingalls Rink. He quotes almost verbatim a harangue by Black Panther David Hilliard — one of the most threatening, violent, and obscene speeches of two weeks that also included much sober reflection and rational discussion. And in his account of the incoherent student who intervened at the rink, he allows the reader to infer that this student's behavior could have been the result of what

Dean Brustein so repeatedly refers to as his being "beaten" and "stomped."

But, in fact, when Dean Brustein telephoned me to verify his hunch that the young man's bizarre behavior resulted from a "concussion" inflicted by the Panthers, I told him that I saw no evidence whatsoever for this hunch — especially since the student's friends had been worried over his psychological condition for weeks before the episode in the rink. I also told Dean Brustein that the young man was repeatedly offered help through the University Health Service, which he refused. By leaving this out, Dean Brustein sustains his imagery of intimidation followed by injury and the acceptance of intimidation.

Dean Brustein's account of the Yale College faculty meeting, again through a series of minor errors, ends up with a serious misrepresentation. He initially establishes his mood of faculty intimidation by referring to "the shouts of students milling on the steps," and by his summary of Kurt Schmoke's remarks. But the students in fact were inaudible during the meeting, while Mr. Schmoke said nothing about the "desperate need for fast support of the student position." He merely said that students were frightened and confused and in need of leadership from the faculty. Furthermore, the resolution introduced by Messers Brooks, Long, and myself did not urge a "redirection" of the University, but only recommended that faculty members have several "options" — the most irregular of which was "postponement of academic exercises and requirements for one week." Dean Brustein does not mention that Professor Bryce LaPorte, who introduced the black faculty resolution, made clear that he planned to continue to meet his classes. As for my amendment to set a terminal date for the modification of "normal academic expectations," Dean Brustein fails to make clear that the amendment was voted upon by the entire faculty and overwhelmingly rejected.

Together these minor omissions and errors lead to a major misrepresentation of the faculty's action. For Dean Brustein indicates the faculty could "in effect, vote away its academic freedom" and "suspend (its) right to teach." This was simply incorrect. He was present at the meeting in which the faculty insisted on its "right to teach," and without a dissenting voice, collectively reaffirmed its commitment to "academic freedom" and non-coercion even in time of crisis.

What in fact happened at Yale was precisely the opposite of Dean Brustein's scenario of intimidation and capitulation. Most faculty members, students, and administrators did not leave town. The university was not intimidated into closing its doors. The faculty did not suspend its right to teach. The university did not

abandon its insistence upon non-coercion, or its determination to resist violence and intimidation. President
Brewster and the administration showed moral courage and leadership; the faculty acted swiftly yet ra-
tionally; and students behaved with admirable calm,
resourcefulness and presence of mind.

The psychological reality of Dean Brustein's own
experience during the two weeks preceding May Day
is undeniable. But to build a dramatization of the two
weeks before May Day around this idiosyncratic experience is to misrepresent — indeed to turn on its
head — what actually happened on the real stage in
New Haven.

Kenneth Keniston,
Professor of Psychology
Yale University School of Medicine
New Haven, Connecticut

Dean Brustein replies:

Dr. Keniston's letter reflects his desire to see the recent
events in New Haven as a splendid educational adventure. Well, the educational insights I made were these:
When a university is forced into a political posture, its
professional functions are inevitably sacrificed, and an

extraordinary amount of intellectual energy can be poured into rationalizing away the memory of panic and violence.

Take that Greek student. After Dr. Keniston led the beaten boy off the platform, promising "to try and help this guy," who was in psychological "trouble," I refrained from commenting on the medical questionableness of such instant psychoanalysis, unsolicited and publicly announced. What I wished to know from Dr. Keniston was how he had followed up on his promise, and whether the student's erratic behavior on the platform could have been caused by a concussion. He did not remember having offered help, said he referred the student (as I wrote) to University Health when the student's friends *later* called him, and assured me that a concussion was not possible on the basis of what he had *later* learned. I therefore made no mention of this conjecture, even by implication, in my article. I had no evidence; by the same token, Dr. Keniston knew nothing of the student's mental state before he saw him for five minutes on the platform. What is most important here is that this student was hustled off a public platform on the pretext that he was going to receive medical attention — an example of what can happen to the practice of psychiatry when it is used for political purposes.

What can happen to the profession of teaching, I have already tried to suggest, and Dr. Keniston's quibbles do not soften the reality of the events. In the faculty meeting, for example, I myself heard the voices of the students on the steps; after all, they were making speeches through a bullhorn less than 200 feet from where we sat. And when a faculty (responding to a call for "leadership" from 1,000 milling students who have already voted to strike) votes to suspend "normal academic expectations" so as to make "as much time as possible available for the discussion of immediate and pressing issues," what else can it be called but a suspension of the right to teach one's subject? Otherwise, why issue a directive on an action that individual teachers could elect freely anyway?

I apologize if I gave others the impression that I was a lonely voice of reason at this time; I plead the pitfalls of personal journalism. But what Dr. Keniston calls my "idiosyncratic experience" was shared by sufficient numbers to result in the departure of an estimated 30 to 40 per cent of the Yale population; and an atmosphere of terror that will be forgotten only by those who wish to lacquer over history. I left because of a lack of sympathy with the demonstration and a hatred of mob action, whether from right or left. If Dr. Keniston failed to see that the threat of violence was real, then this may be because he still has a little myopia in this regard, having written as recently as last year that "the avoidance and control of violence

. . . is a central goal and key psychological orientation in the New Left."

Robert Brustein
R.F.D.
Vineyard Haven, Massachusetts

Dear Bob:

I appreciate your sending me a copy of your letter, replying to mine to the *Times*. And I am sorry that you are at such "a loss to understand a lot of my interpretations and actions these days."

I doubt that the *Times* will be interested in pursuing further our intra-mural squabbles. But for the record, let me clear up one or two continuing misunderstandings shown in your letter to the *Times*.

First, with regard to the controversial "Greek" student. First, I am not, of course, a psychiatrist, and therefore your references to "medical" matters are slightly off the track. But more important, as I believe I told you over the telephone, after helping the student from the platform, I spoke with a number of his friends whom I asked to stick with him throughout

the rest of the evening and the night, and to take him
to the emergency room of the hospital if he appeared
to be endangering himself or others in any way. I also
suggested that they call me at any point if I could be
of any help to them. I heard nothing, but later learned
that the young man had given his friends the slip that
evening. Several days later, one of these friends called
me in mid-morning and asked me to come immediately to the Law School where the Greek student was
apparently attending a class, but continuing to behave
in a bizarre manner. I explained that I could not come
to the Law School before the class ended (because I
was in the midst of an appointment). I suggested,
however, that since it appeared to be an emergency,
the student contact the Department of University
Health. I then immediately telephoned DUH and
spoke to Dr. Arnstein, to whom I explained the situation as I understood it. The student's friend in turn
contacted the psychiatrist on duty that day, and together they worked out a plan involving a concerted
new attempt to make clear to the Greek student that
psychological and medical help was available to him
if he wished to avail himself of it. His friend called
me back and explained the arrangement that had been
made.

Second, as for your charge that I was involved in the
use of the "practice of psychiatry . . . for political
purposes," I find it difficult to understand your con-

clusion that an act motivated by a desire to help another human being whom I perceived as confused, disoriented, and disturbed had a "political purpose." As you should know, I have no special sympathies for the Black Panthers, and would have been delighted had the Greek student spoken coherently against the goings-on on the platform.

Third, as for the "suspension of the right to teach" issue, President Brewster's "directive" to the faculty states "The literal wording as well as the discussion from the floor of the faculty make it clear *there is no desire to urge, let alone require, any faculty member to suspend classes* (my italics)." I fail to see in what way the faculty voted to suspend its right to teach.

Finally, I am delighted that you have been reading *Young Radicals*. Incidentally, it was published two years ago and written in the fall of 1967, not one year ago. But I fear you did not read far enough. See, for example, page 256: "For all his efforts to control violence, cataclysm and sadism, the young radical continually runs the danger of identifying himself with what he seeks to control, and through a militant struggle against violence, creating more violence than he overcomes. The issue of violence is not resolved for these young men and women, nor can it be."

> Sincerely,
> Kenneth Keniston

Kenneth Keniston
Department of Psychiatry
School of Medicine
333 Cedar St.
New Haven, Conn.

Dear Ken:

Thank you for your reply to my letter in the New
York Times. Let me make these final points briefly
in response to your response.

1) Since you are identified as a Professor of Psychiatry
in the Yale School of Medicine, I naturally — and
wrongly — assumed you to be a psychiatrist. Am I
also wrong in assuming that you have patients, and
give therapeutic advice?

2) I do not remember that you told me anything
more than I reported you to have said in my article
and my letter. What you are saying, in effect, is that
after publicly announcing your credentials as a "psychologist," you offered "help" to the Greek student,
and then turned him over to his friends, who somehow lost him. I don't know what "help" means in this
context, except that you "helped" him off the platform,

and then gave some advice about what to do *if* he should later need help.

3) Your interpretation of your action on the platform as "motivated by a desire to help another human being" is only part of the story. As a correspondent wrote to both of us, Why didn't you offer to "help" Hilliard, too? I am not suggesting that your action was motivated by sympathy for the Black Panthers, but rather by a desire to let the meeting proceed without interruption. It was, in short, partly a tactical move, in my opinion, and therefore "political."

4) You miss my point about the right to teach. It is not enough to be permitted to hold classes. The important thing is to hold classes *in your subject* — without moral coercion from university directives, outside picketing, and inside student demands (from those who show up) to deal with "immediate and pressing issues." In my own class, for example, I had hoped to divide the seminar hours between academic work and discussions of the trial, one hour for each. But it was clear halfway through a report on Thomas Middleton (admittedly a pretty dull one) that students would not sit still for anything but debates about the "issues." You must have had the same experience. The fact is the classes became bull sessions

and rap sessions, and the university encouraged this through its directive.

5) I apparently confused the publication date of *The Young Radicals* with that of your article in the Winter 1969 issue of *Dialogue*, called "Youth, Change, and Violence." I apologize for the error, though the latter article shows scant progress in your dawning apprehension that the New Left may be violent, and not some new breed of mankind without frailties or aggression. In the 1969 article, you state: "Although nonviolence as a philosophical principle has lost most of its power in the New Left, nonviolence as a psychological orientation is a crucial — perhaps *the* crucial — issue. The nonviolence of post-modern youth should not be confused with pacifism: these are not necessarily young men and women who believe in turning the other cheek or who are systematically opposed to fighting for what they believe in. But the basic style of the radicals and hippies *is profoundly opposed to warfare, destruction, and exploitation of man by man, and to violence whether on an interpersonal or an international scale.*" (Italics mine). You later say that "It remains to be seen whether . . . their psychological nonviolence will continue to be reflected in their actions," just as you introduce the brief disclaimer you cite in your letter to your other-

wise openmouthed praise of young radicals. But it would be a great deal more helpful to life in general (and to the understanding of our current predicaments) if professionals like yourself, regardless of past mistakes and misinterpretations, would now come forward and examine *dispassionately and without advocacy,* the psychological background for such actions as the explosion on 11th Street and the Chicago Days of Rage. Descriptions of idealism simply will not do, and especially from scientists presumably trained in Freudian techniques. What I am suggesting is that we may have a generation marked by serious character disorders here, and no matter how sympathetic we may be with the political goals of the radicals, it is crucially important to understand the causes of these disorders in order to help prevent them in future. You seem uniquely qualified to undertake such a study.

Sincerely,
Robert Brustein

d. Remarks on "The Vanishing Liberal"

The following is an abridged version of some off-the-cuff remarks made during a symposium on the subject of "The Vanishing Liberal," held under the auspices of The Center for the Study of Democratic Institutions in the summer of 1969. Also on the panel were Harry Ashmore (editor and foundation executive), Murray Kempton (political analyst), Joseph Duffey (former head of the ADA and active in Connecticut politics), Stewart Mott (foundation executive), James Wechsler (Editor of the editorial page, New York Post), and William Thompson, Jr. (Yale student, Class of 1969).

I discovered a few months ago that I was a liberal. All my life I thought I was a radical, and then my radical students informed me that I am really a liberal and that I am responsible for the Vietnam war, the Guatemalan adventure, presumably the Civil War, the extermination of the American Indian, and heaven knows what else. Obviously, the students have preempted radicalism at this point. I think it is incumbent on genuine radicals to try to recapture it from them; it is important not to have to accept their definitions of radicalism.

I do accept the statement that I am a liberal insofar as I reject violent overthrow of the existing government. I also have some distaste, from the aesthetic point of view, for the present student radical style.

146

Can we distinguish between liberals and radical liberals? I think there is a kind of liberal who is guilty of everything the students say he has been guilty of over the last twenty years. I'd like to call him the power liberal, the kind who loves the world and serves it in action, as Yeats put it. Those liberals went into politics to reform things, to make life better, but gradually they found themselves quite often giving high-sounding principles to low actions. Every President of the last twenty-five years, whether Republican or Democrat, has had that kind of liberal around him; some have had five or ten.

I would like to distinguish these liberals from those who make a radical critique of society and have a certain distaste for power and a necessary detachment from it but who stop short of violent overthrow. The radical liberals ought to be further distinguished from the current radicals who are infatuated with power and who, as a result, will be at the mercy of compromise.

We did a play at Yale called "God Bless." Jules Feiffer wrote it, and it illustrates what I am saying here. The liberal in that play was a hundred and ten years old. He had gone through just about everybody's regime. He was very pragmatic. He supported the miners during the miners' strike but turned on the miners when society turned on them. He supported

World War I during the war but was against World
War I when it was over . . . and so forth. There were
also two radicals or revolutionaries in the play who,
to the great despair of the radical students at Yale,
turned out in the end to be just as corrupt as the
liberal. The play was almost disrupted as a result.

I think there is an element of tragic doubt missing
from both the liberal and the radical critique of life.
This doubt was present in the Greeks, and it is also
found in Freud. It is based on the notion that our
natures are biologically determined to be essentially
imperfectible. The radical liberal, that is, the true
liberal, can understand this about man and not be
paralyzed by it. Radicals frequently say that this is
merely an excuse on the part of the radical liberal for
maintaining the status quo. I don't think it is. I believe
it is essential that the tragic sense of life be kept in
mind at the same time that we try to reform life;
otherwise the reformers will become as vicious as the
thing they are trying to reform.

The university is the home of the radical liberal in
the sense that it is and must remain the home of
powerlessness. I want to make a plea to bring the
university back to the ivory tower. I want to urge the
university away from the military-industrial complex.
I want to urge it away, as much as possible, from any
kind of government connections whether in science,

law, drama, what have you. I also want to be consistent and keep it away from the students who want to use it as a base for revolutionizing society. In that sense, the university must be kept out of the world. It must reflect its monastic beginnings; it has to cling to its religious quality. Only in those circumstances can genuinely radical ideas continue to be thought freely. I feel that student radicals, like power liberals, are now preventing genuine radical reform from taking place because they are preventing the ideas that might achieve this reform from being thought. There are really no ideas in the current radical movement. Unless someone starts thinking, the country is going to go down — liberal, radical, reactionary, and all.

e. A Matter of Accountability

The following article appeared on April 18, 1970, in the New York Times.

George Meredith once defined the sentimentalist as "he who would enjoy without incurring the immense debtorship for a thing done" — that is to say, he who gets intoxicated with the sensations of danger without exposing himself to the risks. In this sense, there is certainly a horde of sentimentalists at large in this country today, both within and outside the university. It is a kind of crime against young people to encourage them in the notion that actions have no consequences, and that whatever they feel compelled to do will somehow be greeted with blandness, tolerance, and forgiveness. If you rob a deed of its consequence, you rob it of its possibilities of heroism; you cancel out its importance; you turn it into a facile gesture.

The spectacle of students holding university officials prisoner or of the Young Lords preventing church services from taking place or of the SDS running through high school corridors screaming "Jailbreak" has little of the heroic about it, even when the disruption is committed in the name of equality and justice. But one could more easily grow to respect such behavior were it not always accompanied by the inevitable demands for amnesty. The great difference between the mob actions of our so-called "revolutionaries" and the civil disobedience of a Spock or a Coffin is that the latter is a brave individual act, performed in broad daylight with the hope of changing unjust laws, while the former is merely a rampage, generally in an atmosphere of institutional safety, enacted more for theatrical effect than for social change.

What impresses me most about men like Spock and Coffin, and what distinguishes them from some of the latter-day radicals, is their commitment to passive resistance and non-violence: Like Martin Luther King, from whom they learned their tactics, they manage thereby to create a daily beauty in their lives. Such men function in a world of consequence where, at the risk of official retaliation, they have some chance of making an effect — if not on government policy, then at least on public opinion. The sentimental radicals, on the other hand, who are invariably more violent, enact their scenarios in a university or a church — hardly notorious for war, racism, or repression — which they regard as sanctuaries from the civil authorities, and condemn furiously when they seek to protect themselves.

Whenever such institutions resort to force, they

should be condemned: To invite the police into places devoted to peaceful contemplation is to invite a moral and physical disaster. But even when the university tries to exercise its own sanctions — suspension and expulsion — upon the heels of a violent disruption — even then, it is attacked by a proportion of students and faculty. The demand for accountability, invariably applied to those in positions of authority, is somehow suspended when it comes to the young, so that the university is asked to remain perpetually vulnerable to those who wish to destroy it. For this mechanical application of the concept of amnesty, we have our entire liberal culture to blame, from its child-rearing and education theories through its orientation in the social sciences where we are enjoined to analyze motives, not weigh actions, and to concentrate on causes at the expense of effects. Thus, an idealistic goal can be used to justify any behavior, no matter how fearsome. This is the same kind of reasoning that justifies the conduct of the military in Vietnam on the basis of its efforts to protect democracy in Asia, and excuses the behavior of Mayor Daley or Judge Hoffman because of the "provocations" said to be offered to them.

We must endeavor to keep two ideas in our minds when all the clamoring ideologues are shouting at us to hold only one. Our infatuation with youth has blinded us to the fact that the same generation we have been rightly praising for its idealism is also capable, in extreme moods, of self-justifying righteousness, leading to inexcusable acts of force against others. We are just beginning to see how the violence that has been brutalizing this nation is infecting radicals as well as militarists, and how the virulence of this loathsome war is spreading beyond those who wage it. Recently, some students at the University of Wisconsin stole a Cessna plane and dropped three regulations bombs (fortunately, they were duds) on an Army base. Was this impulse towards indiscriminate slaughter any different from the impulse behind the massacre at Songmy?

The moral superiority of the peace movement is vitiated by those who urge us to "bring the war home," for they are asking us to become one with the very thing we oppose. It is the obligation of those who hate violence to oppose it in any form, even when it wears the mask of an ally. We must beware of those who call others "pig," just as we must beware of those who call others "effete, impudent snobs" — both are dehumanizing the opposition in preparation for committing inhuman acts against it.

Those of us dedicated to resisting illegitimate authority must continually remind ourselves that not all authority is illegitimate. To accept accountability for

our actions, and to demand accountability of others —
young and old, black and white, radical and reactionary
— is to take the first step toward a genuine revolution
of the spirit without which the body of this nation will
not long survive.

f. A Welcoming Speech

The following speech was delivered on September 9, 1969, to the students of the Yale School of Drama.

I want to welcome you to the Yale School of Drama and prepare you a little for what lies ahead. We have, I think, a very distinguished faculty this year. They have come here because of their own professional expertise in the various divisions of the theatre and also because they share, for the most part, the general philosophy of the school. For the school has a decided philosophy which is reflected in the graduation of the first large contingent of Master of Fine Arts and Certificate students into the professional company this year.

This two-way channel between the school and the company has its obvious advantages. It has a limitation as well; and we would do well to face it now. Because the centrality of the company as the end of our training indicates that the main purpose of the school, though not the only purpose, is to prepare students for companies such as our own. This, I should quickly add, is the broadest kind of limitation because the repertory company, which has as its aim the production

155

of both new and classical plays, is the most hospitable place for a wide spectrum of possibilities in the theatre.

As a permanent organism, situated in one place, it does exclude certain things, to be sure. For example, it is not the best place for street or guerilla theatre — but then you don't need much training for that. Certainly you don't need a school. I suspect all you need is a neighborhood or a subway. It's not a gypsy theatre like the Living Theatre, roaming from town to town and university to university. It is not a Grotowski theatre, though it may occasionally use some Grotowski techniques, because the only genuine Grotowski theatre is being run by Grotowski; the rest are poor imitations and without their own personal identity (which is why Grotowski himself repudiates them). It's not even a "poor theatre" in the Grotowski sense, mainly because in a non-socialist country, the only way to pay actors is through the box office and the foundations, until in some unforeseeable future the government decides to subsidize its arts without trying to determine their content. (Even Grotowski can't run a poor theatre in America: At the Brooklyn Academy where the troupe is playing this fall, the tickets are selling for $10 apiece). It is not a black theatre, though it respects and supports the struggle of American black people to achieve equal justice and opportunity in this land. Because one of the ways it sees to do this is to avoid racial limitations or separations of any kind and to open a theatre world in which we are all one.

If it is not any of these things, as a theatre it offers a multitude of possibilities nevertheless for both white and black talents. It aims to be both a classical and a modern theatre, refreshing the past with the present and the present with the past. We believe in a relevant theatre art, but this does not mean a narrowly topical theatre: We do not think relevance is achieved through keeping on top of headlines or in the repudiation of 2,000 years of cultural discovery. If the Second Coming is at hand, it must not be brought about by rough slouching beasts, because only chaos and sterility can result from that. So we believe in cultural continuity, which is to say, neither cultural stagnation, holding on to the past until being dragged kicking and screaming into the present, nor cultural anarchy, in which everything is continually being invented, as if for the first time, and mankind is thought always to be born anew. This means that experiment is essential to our work here, but it does not mean that we must love experiment for its own sake. Experiment is a technique for discovery, not an end in itself. Pasteur's work in the laboratory revolutionized medicine; but how many countless and now anonymous scientists were experimenting with bleeding techniques, full moon sorcery, and dead frogs under pillows before Pasteur's test tubes yielded their significant cultures?

We shall, therefore, encourage experiment at the school and in the company; but we will only honor those experiments that have fruitful results. And the best way to guarantee that experiment has a chance at successful issue is to keep our links with the past. The drama student headed in the direction of our company and companies like ours must therefore be a Janus, a two-headed figure with one face looking forward and the other backward. He must know the great plays and proven production techniques before he ventures into new ground, just as any artisan must know how to handle the old tools before he discovers what new ones to forge. This implies a broad form of training and a versatile individual, open to many possibilities. It also implies an intellectual element in the training and the atmosphere: The capacity to draw on a sizeable body of knowledge and to apprehend it thoroughly before it is rejected or affirmed. And this means the ability to comprehend the aims of others as well as the impulse to explore the self. The great innovators in the theatre always served their apprenticeship before venturing into new territory, if only to learn thoroughly what it was they were opposed to and wished to change: For that reason we are going to ask all of you theatre people to learn your craft thoroughly before seeking to revolutionize it — to build, as Ibsen put it in *The Master Builder*, "castles in the air — but on a firm foundation." This balance is the hardest thing for anyone to maintain; but it is the only balance that has ever produced anything lasting, meaningful and true.

We make some hard demands on you here which you do not always accept with the greatest of pleasure and which you sometimes resist by questioning the quality of the instruction, the direction of the training, or the philosophy of the school. Naturally, these are open to question and will be the subject of continuing debate; but there are certain fundamentals which will not change. It is not easy, in a time which speaks so facilely of liberation, to accept the notion of strict attention to training or absorbing an already created body of knowledge or art. But that is what we stand for here: It is not in tune with the going thing; it runs counter to the current cultural fashions; it is neither voguish, nor modish, nor popular at the moment; it is bucking history, etc. It just happens, in my own opinion, to be the only way we are ever going to get American theatre off the ground, to make it an expression which is neither at the mercy of commercial interests not the interests of the currently fashionable avantgarde, an expression of civilized and humane men. If this country is ever going to have a theatre, it is you who are going to create it. But you won't be able to create very much at all until you are in complete control of all your talents and abilities.

So we believe in training, particularly at the beginning of your work here; and we believe in more and more experimentation when your training has given you the proper tools.

In this activity everybody benefits; the professionals are refreshed by the rejuvenating imagination of younger people; and the students are inspired, both positively and negatively, by the aspirations of the company. I think I can speak for the faculty when I say that the thing that gives us the most pleasure in this work is your achievements and a sense of your continuing development. The supervision exercised by the faculty over your three years is to ensure that this development takes place and is continually encouraged further. But it does mean that you will be supervised, and to some of you, supervision is a restriction on your freedom. I know of no answer to this except to concede the truth of it (though I think most of you know that real freedom in your profession can only be achieved after a period of learning and apprenticeship). And I know of no alternative to supervision by a gifted faculty within the confines of the situation I have outlined.

The importance of the faculty and of faculty supervision in a training situation means that governance must remain in our hands. Yale University is, at present, a largely faculty-run institution. How much more must a conservatory of talent invest the decision-making process in the hands of the teachers of this talent. Because we derive our nourishment in the bosom of a great university, some students tend to confuse our function with that of a liberal arts college or an independent study unit. We bear little relation to that at all.

The faculty and administration intend to consult with you, whenever possible, about school affairs, before reaching decisions that affect you. But we must insist that your role remains advisory and that you accept the decisions that are finally arrived at. I know of no other sensible way to proceed in an artistic situation, without falling into chaos and endless bureaucratic tangles. We are most anxious to have your opinions and suggestions whenever you find it advisable to offer them. We are also anxious to listen to the legitimate grievances that are bound to crop up from time to time; and we are anxious to explore the whole knotty and important question of accountability.

Those of you who are returning know how frequently your suggestions are picked up and acted upon. And I hope we have all sufficiently expressed our gratitude for some of the ideas you have contributed. You also know that many of your suggestions have not been acted upon; and that comes with the territory too. I hope you will always remember, even if some of your opinions are not implemented, that the open exchange continues and will always continue at the school. It cannot continue, however, when suggestions become insistences and opinions harden into demands. One of my most serious character flaws is a certain impatience and impulsiveness. I am not a mellow, avuncular, easily intimidated administrator of the liberal school. And I don't like to be bullied — not even by students for whom I normally feel a great deal of affection — and not even when the bullying is accompanied by the highest professions of idealism. To me, it still adds up to bullying; and it hardly contributes to that atmosphere of mutual respect in which true creative work can only be done.

So if the situation here becomes too intolerable for any of you and you can't find a way to change it short of locking me in my office or heckling faculty members in the classroom, then we will put all the resources of our excellent placement bureau at your command to find you a place somewhere else. I bring this up for the sake of the barely possible, not the probable — I really don't believe that any of you would waste precious creative energy in senseless destructive acts. But I do think it's only fair to forewarn anybody who might be planning, in the contagious atmosphere of the times, a theatrical happening in any of our offices, that we have a scenario for such occasions too, and the faculty is united on this subject.

The most exciting scenarios of this year, however, will be found on our five stages as well as in our classrooms. It is there that the true meaning of a play will become manifest. It is intimately, and paradoxically, tied up with the meaning of work. (Have you ever thought why a drama is called both a play and a work?) Well, as Chekhov says, in each of his plays, "We must work, my friends, we must work." He lived in a time of unhappiness as well — in a time of injustice and inequality, and a time of student unrest, when the possibilities of change seemed remote and faraway; and the age was full of confusion. As an artist, he felt that his purpose was not the solution of problems — that he left to the politicians and the revolutionaries — but rather the correct presentation of the problems. And out of the confusions and contradictions, he forged four beautiful and meaningful works of art that have lasted far longer than anybody's memory of the problems that produced them. But Chekhov was also a deeply compassionate man as well as a brilliant artist. And for those who felt frustrated and anguished by their confusion and powerlessness, he prescribed the panacea of work.

Well, let us work, my friends, let us work — at the same time that we try to counter the narrowness and injustice of our age as best we can in our daily lives. Let us all hope that the fulfilling conjunction of work and play maintains us creatively through the coming years.

g. *A Commencement Address, Yale Drama School, June 8, 1970*

The following address was delivered to the class of 1970 of the School of Drama, and parents, faculty, wives, and friends.

To graduate today is to enter a world of darkness and despair — a world of brutal, unending war abroad, and repression and violence at home. At a time when it seems virtually impossible to have optimistic feelings about anything, however, I think I can at last discern some small advantage in being a graduate of a drama school. It is certainly true that many young graduates today seem affectless and purposeless, torn between withdrawal and destruction, determined to remain outside the American system, if not to find some way to bring it to a conclusion. This is certainly true; but it is also true that regardless of your own political feelings, you have made a decision on behalf of a humane and creative act of life, simply by choosing the theatre as your field of study. For years, people looked on those motivated toward the arts as idle dilettantes in a busy world. This characterization continues to obtain in certain quarters where the artist still lacks honor and

164

prestige and still has difficulty in making a livelihood. Nevertheless, the creative life is rapidly becoming one of the most noble alternatives to our wanton militarism — one of the few options by which our country and our spirits might somehow be redeemed.

We in the theatre are slowly discovering how to be inside and outside the system both at once — how to resist social evils without withdrawing from society itself. For the theatre is both public and private; it involves a confrontation with an audience, and a confrontation with the self; and while it clearly has its social uses, it has never really separated itself from its origins in ritual, and metaphysical consolation. For this reason, the theatre is immensely important in a time of crisis like our own — even when so many people in the theatre are questioning its worth and meaning. Some of you may choose to put your theatre talents at the service of a cause; others have the option of using your talents to remind us that we are civilized men, perpetuating the imagination in a way that demonstrates our failures of breadth and humanity, and providing images towards which men may strive. For if man is a social and political animal, he is also a metaphysical animal with qualities that escape social-political definitions. By telling us about the private, underside of our lives, where we are most often truly ourselves, the artist continues to exercise his supremely important function on behalf of mystery and on behalf of life.

I think it might be appropriate, in this regard, to read some passages from a speech recently made by the novelist, William Styron, before the American Academy of Arts and Letters — a speech in which Styron accepted an award for his novel, *The Confessions of Nat Turner*. Styron's novel is about a great slave hero and the rebellion he began on a Virginia plantation in the 19th Century; and as you may or may not know, the publication of this novel subjected Styron to vilification and abuse by individuals and pressure groups, both black and white, which has dogged him to this day. In this speech, Styron reaffirms the function of the artist at a time when that function is in danger of being forgotten or ignored; and in so doing, rescues not only his own intentions from those who would mangle them for ideological purposes, but also the intentions of all those concerned with creating works of art. I ask you to substitute in your own minds the words *theatre* for *literature*, *drama* for *novel*, and *theatre artist* for *writer*, if you would see how Styron's words apply to our own condition and our own work.

He says:

It seems to me that in honoring my work this award underscores some certainties about the nature of literature. One of these is that a novel worthy of its name is not, nor ever has been, valuable because of its opinions; a novel is speculative, composed of paradoxes and riddles; at its best it is magnificently unopinionated. As Chekhov said, fiction does not provide answers but asks questions — even, I might add, as it struggles to make sense out of the fearful ambiguities of time and history. This award therefore implies an understanding that a novel can possess a significance apart from its subject matter and that the story of a nineteenth century black slave may try to say at least as much about longing, loneliness, personal betrayal, madness, and the quest for God as it does about Negroes or the institution of slavery. It implies the understanding that fiction, which almost by definition is a kind of dream, often tells truths that are very difficult to bear, yet — again as in dreams — is able to liberate the mind through the catharsis of fantasy, enigma and terror.

By recognizing Nat Turner this award really honors all of those of my contemporaries who have steadfastly refused to write propaganda or indulge in mythmaking but have been impelled to search instead for those insights which, however raggedly and imperfectly, attempt to demonstrate the variety, the quirkiness, the fragility, the courage, the good humor, desperation, corruption and mortality of all men. And finally, it ratifies my own conviction that a writer jeopardizes his very freedom by insisting that he be bound or defined by his race, or by almost anything else. For one of the enduring marvels of art is its ability to soar through any barrier, to explore any territory of experience, and I say that only by venturing from time to time into strange territory shall artists, of whatever commitment, risk discovering and illuminating the human spirit that we all share.

I find this statement immeasurably moving and noble — and immensely important at the present time to all of us connected, directly or indirectly, with the making of works of art. For it tells us how, in a bad time, we may continue to serve the spirit of creation. A fragile balance has always existed, in this country, between the demands of our private and our public lives, between our functions as citizens and as solitary, idiosyncratic individuals, between our consciousness of inequality and our urge to exercise the imagination. The Constitution and the Bill of Rights were originally framed to keep that balance steady. For freedom and equality are not essentially compatible ideas; rather, one sometimes threatens the other, if indeed the tension between the two is not an essential condition of living in this country. Now, I believe, this balance is in danger from both the political left and the political right. The left would have us reject all subjects and suppress all truths that do not contribute to a particular political cause, while the right is beginning to attack the rights of free art and a free press, and may, indeed, be preparing to repress all thought that smacks of being critical, dangerous, or non-conformist. I believe that it is just as necessary for us to fight for the preservation of these rights as to fight against social evils in the form of inequality, oppression, and poverty. For us here today, it may even be more important, since these rights constitute our central channel of communication, and have few allies on either side of the political spectrum. As throughout our recent history, it is free expression, artistic possibility, and open scholarship that are caught between the ignorant armies of the night, just as it is the university that is forced, during crisis, to conform to the demands of its most clamorous elements, and serve a single point of view.

The insistence on the right to create — as independently, as oddly, as irrelevantly as he wants — is the fundamental imperative of the artist. And we will have failed in our own purposes here if, along with whatever skills and powers you may have developed at the Yale

School of Drama, you do not carry away with you this single and overriding imperative.

Finally, I would like to say, on behalf of the entire faculty and staff, that we are very very regretful to let you go, and we sincerely hope that you will never let go of us. Yale has been a kind of home to you over the past three years, in both an artistic and more personal sense, and it has probably evoked in you all the complicated feelings that go along with home. You have changed this home, and I think it has changed you as well; and so there is something organic and growing here that you have left, a part of you, that will still be recognizable in future times. I hope that in the ensuing years, whatever complications you may feel towards us will disappear, leaving you with good strong memories of those who have grown with you, and through you — and to whom you will always be welcome in the community of art.

ABOUT THE AUTHOR

Robert Brustein, contributing editor of the *New Republic,* is the author of several volumes of critical opinion on the theatre. *The Third Theatre,* a collection of reviews and essays, was published in 1969; *Seasons of Discontent,* a volume of dramatic opinion, in 1965; *The Theatre of Revolt,* a study of the modern drama, in 1964. In addition, Mr. Brustein has contributed to the following volumes: *The Plays of Strindberg* (1964); and *The Plays of Chekhov* (1964).

Mr. Brustein has been the recipient of grants from the Guggenheim and Ford foundations and has been granted the honorary degree of Doctor of Letters from Lawrence University (1968). He has served on the faculties of Cornell, Vassar, Columbia, and Yale, where he is Dean of the School of Drama. He is forty-three years old and lives in New Haven with his wife and two sons.